# ALEXANDER II
## AND THE
## MODERNIZATION OF RUSSIA

*perform in all its newness*

"The Tsar Who Lost
Control"

# ALEXANDER II

## and the

# Modernization of Russia

### W. E. MOSSE

*Professor Emertitus of European History,*
*University of East Anglia*

I.B. Tauris & Co Ltd
*Publishers*
London • New York

Published in 1992 by I.B. Tauris & Co Ltd
110 Gloucester Avenue, London NW1 8JA

175 Fifth Avenue
New York, NY 10010

In the United States of America
and Canada distributed by
St. Martin's Press, 175 Fifth Avenue
New York, NY 10010

An edition of this book was published by the English Universities
Press in the series Men and Their Times in 1958.

A CIP record for this book is available from the British Library

Library of Congress catalog card number available
A full CIP record is available from the Library of Congress

ISBN 1-85043-513-8 hardback
ISBN 1-85043-512-x paperback

# Contents

Dates are given according to our present Gregorian Calendar. In Alexander's day, Russians used the Julian Calendar which was then twelve days behind the Gregorian. Where it was desirable to give a date in both styles, they have been placed side by side.

# INTRODUCTION = easy to date
## pessimistic

The story of Alexander II, Tsar of All Russia from 1855 until 1881, is not without relevance for an understanding of contemporary events in what used to be the Soviet Union. Alexander II, known to history as 'The Tsar Liberator', was the originator of an earlier form of *perestroika*, the so-called 'Great Reforms'. At the centre of these reforms was the Liberation of the Serfs in 1861. Alexander also transformed the judicial system, set up new institutions of local self-government and gave a wide autonomy to the newly reorganized universities. Under him, an enlightened Minister of War introduced a system of universal conscription and remodelled the Russian army. As part of a policy of greater *glasnost*, Alexander relaxed the 'censorship-terror' of the previous reign. National and religious minorities benefited from more enlightened policies. In the economic sphere, the construction of major railway lines gave Russia an infrastructure that would form the basis for early industrialization. At the same time, a long-serving Minister of Finance tried, with indifferent success, to pave the way for an overdue currency reform. Few aspects of Russian life remained untouched by Alexander's *perestroika*. In general, an element of dynamism was introduced into a hitherto stagnant society. Russia's archaic ancien regime underwent at least a partial modernization. Though the country would in the end emerge as a hybrid society uneasily combining the old and the new, it was to be set firmly on the path to modernization. The 'Great Reforms' of

Alexander II marked Russia's first steps on the road to a 'de-feudalized', bourgeois-capitalist society.

In important respects the 'Great Reforms' of Alexander II can be compared to the *perestroika* of the late 1980s and early 1990s. Both sprang from similar causes, deeply embedded in Russian history. The tasks facing the reformers were comparable, as were the obstacles they encountered. The partial achievements also bear comparison. In fact, both *perestroika*s are instances of a recurring phenemenon of modern Russian history: the hectic attempt at 'modernization' following a period of stagnation. The motivation for the reforms of Peter the Great, Alexander II's 'Great Reforms', Stalin's Five Year Plans and Gorbachev's *perestroika* show comparatively little variation over the centuries. In this respect at least the October Revolution marks less of a break than has sometimes been supposed. Similar deep-seated causes, in effect, produce similar results and are likely to do so in the future. Awareness of these causes is the key to an understanding of modern Russia and its history. They form the framework within which the career and achievement of Alexander II must be seen. They help to explain both the successes and the failures of the *perestroika* he set in motion. *Perestroika*, the attempt at accelerated modernization, is the product of several basic factors. One of these is Russia's backwardness, her poverty, low productivity and overall economic underdevelopment. 'The fundamental and most stable feature of Russian history,' wrote Leon Trotsky,[1] 'is the slow tempo of her development, with economic backwardness, primitiveness of social forms and low level of culture resulting from it.' He continued:

> The population of this gigantic and austere plain, open to Eastern winds and Asiatic migration, was condemned by nature itself to a long backwardness. The struggle with nomads lasted almost to the end of the seventeenth century; the struggle with winds, bringing winter cold and summer drought, continues still. Agriculture, the basis of the whole

development, advanced by extensive methods. In the north they cut down and burned up the forests, in the south they ravished the virgin steppes. The conquest of nature went wide and not deep.

Muscovy/Russia lacked the cultural heritage bequeathed by Rome to western societies:

> While the Western barbarians settled in the ruins of Roman culture, where many an old stone lay ready as building material, the Slavs in the East found no inheritance upon their desolate plain: their predecessors had been on an even lower level of culture than they. The Western European peoples, soon finding their natural boundaries, created those economic and cultural clusters, the commercial cities. The population of the Eastern plain, at the first sign of crowding, would go deeper into the forest or spread out over the steppe.

Russia lacked urban development of the kind found in the West.

> The meagreness not only of Russian feudalism, but of all the old Russian history, finds its most depressing expression in the absence of real medieval cities as centres of commerce and craft. Handicraft did not succeed in Russia in separating itself from agriculture, but preserved its character of home-industry. The old Russian cities were commercial, administrative, military and manorial – centres of consumption consequently, not of production.

Such trade as did develop in Russia was unlike that in the West:

> . . . nomad traders could not possibly occupy that place in social life which belonged in the West to the craft-guild and merchant-industrial petty and middle bourgeoisie, inseparably bound up with its peasant environment. The chief roads of Russian trade, moreover, led across the border, thus from time immemorial giving the leadership access to foreign commercial capital, and imparting a semi-colonial character to the whole process in which the Russian trader was a mediator between the Western cities and the Russian villages. This kind of economic relationship developed further during the epoch of Russian capitalism and found its extreme expression in the imperialist war.

The insignificance of the Russian cities 'more than anything else promoted the development of an Asiatic state, also made impossible a Reformation – that is, a replacement of the feudal-bureaucratic orthodoxy by some sort of modernized kind of Christianity adapted to the demands of bourgeois society.'

To his list of Russian handicaps Trotsky might have added others. Not least among these was an unfavourable geographical location which effectively cut Russia off from the principal avenues of overseas trade. This was compounded by a lack of ice-free ports. Not for Russia, therefore, the lucrative colonial trade, the wealthy commercial emporia with their banking and maritime insurance, their ship-building and privateering, industrial production and early capital-formation.[2] Another impediment to development was two centuries of Tartar domination (*c.* 1240-1480) which cut Muscovy/Russia off from the rest of Europe and subjected it to heavy exactions, destructive raids and the payment of tribute to the Tartar Khans. Yet another influence retarding Russian development was the other-wordly philosophy of the Russian Orthodox Church with its spiritual rather than material concerns.

Last but not least, there was the character of the Russian people. 'The Czar of Muscovia, although a Christian, rules a lazy-minded people,' Giovanni Battista Vico wrote early in the eighteenth century[3] In the nineteenth, the writer Ivan Goncharov created his immortal anti-hero Oblomov, characterized by impeturbable indolence and reluctance to involve himself in any form of activity. Many Russians admitted the justice of the description. Lenin, in the twentieth century, castigated and lamented his countrymen's incurable *Oblomovshchina*.

Many factors were thus responsible for Russia's underdevelopment. In a report to the tsar at the end of the nineteenth century, the Minister of Finance, Sergei Witte, wrote:

> Russia remains even at the present essentially an agricultural country. It pays for all its obligations to foreigners by exporting raw materials, chiefly of an agricultural nature, principally grain. It meets its demand for finished goods by imports from abroad. The economic relations of Russia with Western Europe are fully comparable to the relations of colonial countries with their metropolises . . . (4)

In 1960, a political scientist wrote:

> The Soviet Union today . . . is a semi-developed country; only the heavy industrial sector of the economy is fully developed, only one sector of Soviet society, the technocracy fully advanced. The rest of the country is underdeveloped. (5)

And in 1991, the head of Estonia's national bank observed wistfully: 'Our entire industry is obsolete. What can we sell abroad?'(6)

Yet notwithstanding her feeble economic base, Russia, thanks largely to size, numbers and not least foreign assistance, had for centuries been a substantial power. From a Baltic power she had developed into a European and, finally, a world power. As Witte observed, in spite of her quasi-colonial economic relationship with the West, there was still a great difference between Russia and a colony:

> Russia is an independent and strong power. She has the right and the strength not to want to be the eternal handmaiden of states which are more developed economically. (7)

Stalin, in 1931, dwelt on the implications of backwardness for Russia's international standing:

> One feature of the history of old Russia was the continual beatings she suffered for falling behind, for her backwardness. She was beaten by the Mongol Khans. She was beaten by the Turkish beys. She was beaten by the Swedish feudal lords. She was beaten by the Polish and Lithuanian gentry. She was beaten by French and British capitalists. She was beaten by the Japanese barons. All beat her – for backwardness, for military backwardness, for cultural backwardness, for political

backwardness, for industrial backwardness. She was beaten because to beat her was profitable and went unpunished. [8]

And Stalin concluded: 'We are fifty or a hundred years behind the advanced countries. We must make good this lag in ten years. Either we accomplish this or we will be crushed.' [9] To 'catch up' with and even to 'overtake' the more advanced countries had become the perennial ambition of Russian rulers from the days of Peter the Great to our own. But how to achieve this goal? *Perestroika* – modernization – was clearly the only path. After the Crimean *débâcle,* for instance, modernization alone seemed the way to restore Russia's shaken prestige, to enable her to preserve her international standing. An attempt had to be made to overcome her backwardness. It was yet another case of 'challenge and response'; it had occurred before and would occur in the future.

No *perestroika* was possible without assistance from 'the West', from Russia's potential rivals in international competition. The need to modernize thus raised the complex question of Russia's ambivalent relationship with the more advanced countries. Having to co-exist and indeed to compete with these nations was an ineluctable fact of Russian history.

The more advanced nations of the West differed from Muscovy/Russia in important respects. There are differences, in religious observances, in world-views and culture, skills and attainments, in life-styles and living standards. In spite of persistent attempts by Russian governments to shelter their subjects from Western 'contagion', such a policy could never be wholly successful. One reason was the inescapable Russian dependence on foreign expertise in a great variety of fields. Moreover, since the time of Peter the Great there had existed a constant temptation, in spite of the risks, to send young Russians to study at foreign institutions. Muscovy/Russia in spite of all efforts could never be turned into a hermetically sealed society.

The reaction of most educated Russians to their encounter with 'the West' was always ambivalent. Its superiority in many spheres was recognized by all. Yet some, perhaps a majority, recognized this with reluctance. Others, considering Russia an essentially barbarous country, embraced the Western model wholeheartedly. The different reactions in the nineteenth century led to a deep ideological split between 'slavophiles' and 'Westernizers'. Whilst the former dwelt on the alleged superiority of Russian Orthodoxy, with its spiritual values, over the 'rotten West', with its dry legalism, materialism and atheism (or at best Protestant rationalism), the Westernizers in their turn castigated Russian barbarism and backwardness. Whilst slavophiles sang the praises of traditional Russian institutions, Orthodoxy, autocracy, the idealized village commune or *mir*, the spirit of *sobornost*,[10] Westernizers wished to replace them by 'Western' constitutionalism, civil rights and a régime of *glasnost*.

The division of Russian opinion inevitably influenced attitudes to *perestroika*. No 'restructuring' was possible without a large measure of borrowing from the West. There was no other available 'role model'. This made *perestroika* almost synonymous with 'Westernization'. Welcomed by Westernizers, it is highly uncongenial to slavophiles who, nevertheless, could not deny its necessity. They were also forced to admit that to maintain Russia's standing among the nations there was 'no other way'.

Whilst the division of slavophiles and Westernizers was primarily ideological (or philosophical), the two clashed in practice over legislation involving matters like the village commune or the respective roles of Church and state in elementary education. They differed also over attempts by reformers to modify or abolish the institution of autocracy. Only where *perestroika* would either remedy crying abuses or could be seen as a practical necessity would it become acceptable to slavophile opinion.

*Perestroika*, except on rare occasions when it was in part a response to pressure from below, as a rule originated from the top. It was the work of an absolute ruler, assisted by a reforming minority within the ubiquitous bureaucracy. Only 'strong' central government could overcome the resistance of vested interests favoured by the apathy or inertia of 'the masses'. In any event, no *perestroika* was likely to succeed without concessions to conservative opponents. Reforms were watered down either during the legislative process itself or in the course of their application. Only firm determination of those in authority, the prestige of the ruler and at time a measure of tactical skill could overcome the powerful twin forces of obstruction and inertia.

*Perestroika* invariably destablized the existing order. Far-reaching changes created an atmosphere of uncertainty and unrest. *Perestroika* whetted the appetite of some whilst at the same time mobilizing the forces of resistance. In addition to splitting the 'upper classes', it also resulted in disorders, violence and even terrorism.

Faced with growing unrest and with attacks from both right and left, the 'middle of the road' reformer became weary. After a time, the major part of any *perestroika* was in any case completed, at least in its legislative aspect. *Perestroika* then lost its momentum and gradually fizzled out. At the same time, the unrest it provoked provided a golden opportunity for the 'law and order' men. The early result was a hybrid administration with reformers in charge of technical ministries and 'policemen' controlling the security apparatus. From a struggle with forces of opposition there emerged a new repressive régime.

The new institutions created by *perestroika* were meanwhile integrated – imperfectly – into the older system. The old and new then existed uneasily side by side. What emerged, whilst different from the old order was not the 'brave new world' dreamt of by some reformers. The reformers themselves either abandoned their earlier liberalism, were killed or lost their influence. They often suffered sad endings. Yet the achievements of *perestroika*, though sometimes emasculated, were never wholly wiped out and there was no direct restoration of the old order. However, pending the emergence of the next challenge, Russian society sank back into its state of near-stagnation and apathy.

*Perestroika* is often associated with another cyclical phenomenon observable in Russian history, the alternation of long periods of political repression and, usually short-lived, 'thaws'. The transition from one to the other often followed a change of ruler. After the more or less 'sticky' end of the old 'tyrant', a more youthful successor would partially dismantle his predecessor's repressive apparatus and introduce for a time a régime of 'quasi-liberal' *glasnost*.

The 'thaw' sometimes formed the prelude to a period of *perestroika*, when small groups of relatively youthful reformers sought to transform Russian institutions and society. The attempt, as already indicated, provoked unrest which in turn 'triggered' a conservative backlash. The newly aroused claims of various nationalities created additional problems. So did international complications. At the same time the 'law and order' men restricted the area of *glasnost* and replaced the 'thaw' with a period of 'semi-repression'. Under the impact of some major upheaval, revolt, assassination or revolution, a fully repressive régime was installed – after which the cycle could recommence.

'Thaws' were as a rule accompanied by an increase of

*glasnost*. Censorship was relaxed. Greater freedom was allowed for the expression of critical opinions. Government policies could be scrutinized and even criticized without fear of instant reprisals. Information about government plans was made more readily available. The 'public' might even be consulted about proposed legislation. Restrictions on foreign contacts were relaxed. The security services were subjected to some restraint. Under the impact of *glasnost*, publications multiplied, some with an oppositional or even a revolutionary bent. Academic institutions developed into centres of radical thought. 'Dissent' began to create rudimentary networks. Opposition leaders preached further radical change. Some called for the overthrow of the government. Public opinion, unshackled by *glasnost*, was perceived by the authorities as a threat, particularly where radicals turned from words to deeds.

The relation between *glasnost* and *perestroika* was thus a curious one. *Glasnost* and attendant manifestations strengthened the conservative backlash and played into the hands of 'anti-reformers'. Some reformers also saw in *glasnost* an obstacle to reform. Reforms could on occasion be introduced and made effective only by the use of emergency powers, the right to govern by decree. Such powers, however, could easily lead to a curtailment of *glasnost*. So far as *perestroika* is concerned, *glasnost*, by weakening or distracting the central power was frequently 'disfunctional'.

Yet, without at least some element of *glasnost*, *perestroika* of necessity remained a bureaucratic construct, elaborated by desk-bound *chinovniks* (higher and middle-ranking officials) in the distant capital. It thus bore little relation to local realities. The implications and effects of proposed reforms were imperfectly understood at the centre. *Glasnost*, at any rate in theory, formed a useful corrective. However, given a diversity of views, it was in the absence of consensus of little assistance to the reforming legislator. Indeed, far from helping, it was a retarding influence.

Thus, whilst *glasnost* might be a desirable object in itself, it was difficult to maintain that it was a necessary adjunct of *perestroika*. The two were distinct and partly independent phenomena. Economic *perestroika* in particular was feasible without *glasnost* or democracy. In relation to *perestroika*, *glasnost* could be considered a neutral influence potentially benefiting in equal measure protagonists and opponents of reform.

It is within the parameters of these wider factors of Russian history that the life and career of the 'Tsar Liberator' must be seen. His reign, in fact, illustrates most of the features which have been described. It provides a basis for comparison with the cases of other Russian reformers. 'All cases,' says T.S. Eliot (in a very different context), 'are unique and very similar to others.' The attentive reader will note parallels (and of course some differences) between the 'Great Reforms' of Alexander II and subsequent attempts at 'restructuring'. They help to underline the continuity of Russian history across the sometimes over-rated 'great divide', of the October Revolution. Bolshevism like tsarism before it could neither abolish nor resolve the basic problems of Russian history or their causes. These persist to the present day and will almost certainly continue to do so. Whilst the 'Great Reforms' throw light on some problems facing present-day reformers, contemporary experience in its turn illuminates the experience of Alexander II. It is this double relationship which in some repects makes Alexander II a contemporary figure worthy of study.

Moreover, the examination of successive *perestroika*s, not least that of Alexander II, also has a predictive value. Alexander's 'Great Reforms' cannot be termed a complete success. His liberation of the serfs did not solve Russia's agrarian problem but merely changed its nature. Neither did the *zemstva* as they gradually emerged completely fulfil earlier expectations. The reformed judicial system, a great improvement on the old, nevertheless retained a number of its weaknesses. Dimitri Miliutin's reformed army failed to win glory in either the Russo-Turkish or the Japanese wars. Altogether, the 'brave new Russia' that emerged from the 'Great Reforms' preserved many characteristics of the old which no *perestroika* could eradicate. Alexander II died a violent death, a disappointed, disillusioned and widely unloved man.

Yet at the same time, his 'Great Reforms' ushered in changes which would in their long-term effect prove revolutionary. They contributed significantly to both the 'modernization' and the Westernization of Russia. A 'feudal' agricultural society was set on the road to becoming in time a bourgeois-capitalist one. From being an essentially static society, Russia was transformed into one showing elements of dynamism.

Yet the overall object of Alexander's *perestroika*, as of those of his successors, would never be fully attained. Russia's relative backwardness could not be overcome. What is true of the 'Great Reforms' probably applies in equal measure to current attempts at re-structuring. In the light of past experience, including that of Alexander II, it seems safe to predict that, whilst major changes may be introduced, the ultimate objective will forever prove elusive. There will be other, partially successful *perestroika*s which will not succeed in radically altering the basic situation. It is, for the reasons discussed, Russia's historic destiny to 'lag behind'. At the deepest level, Russia would appear to be 'unreformable'. That is the tragedy of Alexander II as perhaps of other would-be reformers. It is the conclusion to be drawn (and, possibly, the lesson to be learnt) from the story of the Tsar-Liberator and his 'Great Reforms'.

(1) For the following see Leon Trotsky, *The History of the Russian Revolution* (London, 1932) I, pp.23-27

(2) The commercial success of Novgorod the Great in the Hanseatic League was shortlived and brought to a violent end by Muscovite expansionism. It would in any case have withered with the commercial decline of the Baltic.

(3) Quoted in Trotsky, *op. cit.* p.23

(4) T.H. Von Laue, "Sergei Witte on Industrialization of Imperial Russia", *The Journal of Modern History* XXVI, no. 1 (1964), p.66

(5) F. Parkinson "Social Dynamism of Under-developed Countries", in *Year Book of World Affairs* 1960 vol. 14 p.230

(6) Quoted in *Newsweek* Sept 9th, 1991 p.11

(7) T.H. Von Laue, *loc. cit.*

(8) Quoted in T.H. Von Laue, *Why Lenin? Why Stalin?* (New York, 1964), p.211

(9) Quoted *ib.* p.212

(10) An untranslatable term with semi-mystic overtones derived from *sobor* (cathedral) 'Cathedral-ness', the spirit of the congregation, could be translated clumsily as 'worshipfulness' or inadequately as 'piety'.

pessimistic

'Experience shows that the most dangerous moment for a bad government is usually when it begins to reform itself.'
—ALEXIS DE TOCQUEVILLE

'No despot can make happy a country which his predecessors have made unhappy. The traces left by centuries of oppression cannot be wiped out by imperial decree. That is the tragedy of Alexander II.'—KURD VON SCHLÖZER

# Preface

WHILE the names of Peter the Great and Lenin have become household words, that of Alexander II, Emperor of all the Russias from 1855 until his assassination in 1881, is familiar only to the specialist. Yet the 'Tsar Liberator' is associated with a social transformation hardly inferior in importance to the reforms of Peter or Lenin's October Revolution. B. H. Sumner says : "The emancipation of the serfs (1861) and the other reforms of the sixties marked the watershed between the old and the nineteenth-century Russia, much as the reign of Peter the Great marked that between the old Muscovy and the New Russia." [1] In spite of his less dynamic personality, Alexander II deserves to rank with the two great innovators among the makers of modern Russia.

If the effect of Alexander's reign is to be summed up in a single phrase, it may be said to mark the transition in Russia from a semi-feudal to an early capitalist economy. Two measures in particular helped to accelerate the process. The liberation of the serfs increased the available force of mobile free labour. The construction of railways stimulated the growth of Russian industry. Together with a great expansion of banking and credit facilities, these developments laid the foundations of an 'Industrial Revolution' which has continued without intermission until the present day.

The economic transformation of Alexander's reign

[1] B. H. Sumner, *Survey of Russian History* (second revised edn., London, 1947), p. 352.

found its reflection in the social sphere. The liberation of the serfs accelerated the decline of the landowning nobility. It assisted the more prosperous peasants but hastened the pauperization of the poorer. At the same time the expansion of Russian industry swelled the numbers of the industrial proletariat. The progress of banking and commerce increased the importance of capitalist entrepreneurs. In their cumulative effect these changes undermined the position of the gentry in Russian social life.

This development in its turn had political repercussions which received a measure of recognition in Alexander's administrative reforms. The abolition of seigneurial jurisdiction reduced the authority of landowners over their peasants. The creation of all-class zemstvos destroyed the administrative monopoly of officialdom and gentry. By the introduction of conscription, the theoretical equality of all the Tsar's subjects in the matter of military service was recognized. A radical reform of the law-courts and the adoption of the jury system reduced the power of the bureaucracy. Finally, a relaxation of the censorship regulations allowed the growing intelligentsia to engage in the public discussion of political questions. Russian political journalism, and with it the growing influence of 'public opinion', date essentially from the time of Alexander II.

For these reasons, it seems hardly too much to say that Alexander II carried out a revolution from above as important in its effects as the movements which in 1848 had elsewhere called students and workers to the barricades. By his autocratic power he gave Russia what the United States of America won only after four years of bloody civil war. Moreover, if Russia, after her defeat in the Crimea, was able to maintain her position as a European power, she owed this in no small measure to the reforms carried out under his direction. The Great Reforms make Alexander II an important figure in the history of nineteenth-century Europe.

# ALEXANDER II
## AND THE
## MODERNIZATION OF RUSSIA

## Chapter One

# Unreformed Russia

WHEN Alexander II ascended the throne in 1855 Russia, by European standards, was a poor and backward country. Of the sixty million inhabitants of European Russia (excluding the non-Russian fringes), some fifty million were peasants. As against this, the number of workers employed in industry was insignificant. In 1825, there had been some 210,000 industrial workers. By 1855 their numbers had risen to about 483,000. Of these many still returned to their native villages for the harvesting season. Well over nine-tenths of the people lived permanently in the villages. Commercially, Russia was undeveloped. In 1847, when the value of her exports reached 134 million rubles, the share of purely Russian firms was less than 2 per cent. The rest was in the hands of foreign or predominantly foreign firms. Communications were rudimentary. The condition of the roads was deplorable. Railways were in their infancy. A proposal in 1835 to build a comprehensive network of railways had been opposed by the Minister of Finance on the grounds that it was unnecessary, costly, and a danger to 'public morals'. Railways encouraged 'frequent purposeless travel, thus fostering the restless spirit of our age'. None the less, the first line, totalling only 16½ miles,[1] was opened at this time. The first major line, that linking St. Petersburg and Moscow, was constructed between 1842 and 1851 by American engineers with

[1] The Russians measured their distances in *versts*. One verst equals 0·66 mile.

American capital. In consequence, Russia, by 1855, could boast of a grand total of some six hundred and fifty miles of railway.

The major symptom of Russian backwardness was the persistence of personal bondage or serfdom. In 1835, some 10·9 million *male* serfs lived on estates belonging to the hereditary nobility, whilst another 10·6 million were settled on state lands. In 1859, their numbers were about 10·7 and 12·8 million respectively. In that year serfs of both groups, together with their families, numbered above 40 million. Agricultural serfdom imposed on the serf a heavy economic burden. Of the land belonging to an estate, he was allowed to cultivate a part for his own use. The remainder was farmed directly by the landowner or the local administrator of state property. For the share of the land which he was allowed to farm for himself, the serf was obliged to make to the landowner (whether a squire or the state) a payment in cash or in labour. The first was known as *obrok*, the second as *barshchina*. The geographical distribution of the two forms of payment varied. Where a proprietor had an abundance of fertile land which he wished to farm on his own account, he would demand from his serfs as much labour as possible. Where, on the contrary, he had at his disposal more servile labour than was needed to cultivate his own fields, he would put the superfluous serfs on *obrok*—that is to say, he would allow them to go and work wherever they wished in return for a fixed yearly payment. The first case was common in the fertile grain-producing provinces south of Moscow, the second in the barren regions of north-eastern Russia. A special group of landowners' serfs were the houseserfs, described with much justification as 'domestic slaves rather than serfs in the proper sense of the term'. Their number, which during the first half of the nineteenth century was steadily increasing, may by 1855 have reached a million and a half.

The legal power of the owner over his serfs was subject to no effective limitation or control. "The owner", said the law, "may impose on his serfs every kind of labour, may take from them money dues and demand from them personal service, with this restriction, that they should not thereby be ruined, and that the number of days fixed by law should be left to them for their own work." The last proviso referred to a law of 1797 limiting the maximum of *barshchina* to three days a week and confining it to week-days. These provisions were difficult to enforce. Whilst three days of *barshchina* a week were normal, four and even five days were not unknown. Moreover, the distribution of the labour days owed to the lord was nowhere clearly defined. Some owners during the short ploughing and harvesting seasons would force their serfs to work continuously on the home farm to the neglect of their own plots.

The economic exploitation of the serfs was backed by the power of the state. For any offence committed against himself or anyone under his jurisdiction, the owner was permitted by law to inflict on his serf a punishment not exceeding forty lashes with the birch or fifteen blows with a stick. In actual fact, none of the serfs and very few of the proprietors knew that the law placed any sort of restriction upon the right of chastisement. No limits were observed in practice. So long as the proprietor refrained from the habitual practice of inhuman cruelty, the authorities never thought of interfering. Flogging in the stables was accepted as a common feature of Russian village life; in the towns it formed part of the regular duties of the police and the fire-brigade. Infinitely more dreadful to the serf than either birch or stick was the owner's right to present him to the authorities either as a recruit or for transportation to Siberia. It was assumed, in theory, that such punishments would be resorted to only in extreme cases; in fact, the authorities accepted without question any serf presented to them. The owner's threat to enrol a serf as a soldier was an instrument of blackmail and extortion which rarely failed of its purpose. Finally, where an owner had driven his serfs to insubordination or mutiny, he had the legal right to call in the police and the military to restore order. Such punitive expeditions, as a rule, ended in an orgy of floggings.

Such were the economic and legal aspects of serfdom. What the institution meant in terms of human suffering and degradation is hard to describe in words. For the ordinary peasant, serfdom meant a life of backbreaking work, grinding poverty, dirt, ignorance, and superstition. It meant utter subjection to the whims of owners and their stewards, brutal floggings and cringing servility, relieved by occasional drunken orgies as the only means of escape. The domestic serf often led a lazy, idle existence, but on the other hand he was in closer relation with an often brutal and always tyrannical master. Serf girls and women, particularly, suffered the consequences of their subjection. The case of the landowner in south-western Russia who claimed the literal fulfilment of the *ius primæ noctis* was, no doubt, an exception. However, all accounts of the period agree that in their dealings with serf girls and women the majority of Russian landowners knew little or no restraint. "Half the landowners killed by their serfs", wrote Alexander Herzen, a shrewd observer of the Russian scene, "die for their deeds of valour on the field of love." Peter Kropotkin, 'repentant nobleman', sensitive offspring of an old princely family, after recording in his memoirs some of the things which he saw in his father's house, continues :

"These were things which I myself saw in my childhood. If, however, I were to relate what I heard of in those years it would be a much more gruesome narrative : stories of men and women torn from their families and their villages and sold, or lost in gambling, or exchanged for a couple of hunting dogs, and then transported to some remote part of Russia for the sake of creating a new estate; of children taken from their parents and sold to cruel or dissolute masters; of flogging 'in the stables', which occurred every day with unheard of cruelty; of a girl who found her only salvation in drowning herself; of an old man who had grown grey-haired in his master's service and at last hanged himself under his master's window; and of revolts of serfs, which were suppressed by Nicholas I's generals by flogging to death each tenth or fifth man taken out of the ranks, and by laying waste the village, whose inhabitants, after military execution, went begging for bread in the neighbouring provinces, as if they had been the victims of a conflagration. As to the poverty which I saw during our journeys in certain villages, especially in those which belonged to the imperial family, no words would be adequate to describe the misery to readers who have not seen it."

No serf could marry without the owner's consent. What is more, he must, if ordered, marry the person selected for him. Kropotkin describes an instance—one landowner once asked another : "Why is it, General, that the number of souls [male peasants] on your estate increases so slowly? Probably you don't look after their marriages." A few days later, the general called for a list of the inhabitants of his village. He picked out the names of all young men who had just attained the age of eighteen and of the girls just past sixteen—the legal ages for marriage in Russia. Then he wrote on a slip of paper: "John to marry Anna, Paul to marry Parashka", and so on with five couples. The weddings must take place in ten days' time, the following Sunday but one. A cry of despair rose from the village. Women young and old wept in every house. Anna had hoped to marry Gregory; Paul's parents had already talked to the Fedotovs about their girl. In any case, this was the season for ploughing not weddings, and what wedding could be prepared in ten days? Dozens of peasants came to see the landowner; their womenfolk took pieces of fine linen to his wife to secure her intercession. It was of no avail. The master had fixed the date of the weddings, and so it must be. On the appointed day, the processions made their way to church, the women wailing as they did at funerals. Parashka refused to be married to Paul. The squire, informed of the fact, sent a messenger to the priest: "Tell that long-maned drunkard [the Russian priests wore their hair long and, on occasion, were not averse to drink] that if Parashka is not married at once, I will report him to the archbishop as a drunkard. . . . Tell him he will be sent to rot in a monastery and that I will exile Parashka's family to the steppes." When the message was delivered, Parashka's mother fell on her knees, imploring her daughter not to ruin the whole family. Parashka continued saying "I won't", but in a weakening voice, until at last she stood silent. The nuptial crown was placed on her head and she made no further resistance.

Not every Russian landowner—they numbered a quarter of a million—was either a monster or a libertine. Cases of sadism and inhuman cruelty, although far from infrequent, were exceptional. But even in 'normal' conditions, serfdom was sad enough. Old Prince Alexis Kropotkin was neither vicious nor particularly brutal; his serfs and his servants classed him among the better masters. His son recorded some incidents in his household. The maid Polya (Pauline) had been taught to make fine embroidery and become an artist at her work. She had been given some education, and become a companion rather than a housemaid. When it became apparent that Pauline was going to have a child, her furious mistress had her hair cut short and exiled her to the dairy. The father of the child, serf of another landowner, implored permission to marry her. As he had no money to offer, his request

16

was refused. In the meantime, another husband had been selected for Polya. 'Bandy-legged Filka' had as a child been kicked by a horse and had not properly grown. His legs were crooked, his feet turned inwards, his nose was broken, and his jaw deformed. To Filka, the unhappy Polya was married by force, after which the couple were sent away to work as peasants on one of the prince's estates.

Gerasim Kruglov had been educated at the prince's expense at the Moscow Agricultural Institute. A brilliant pupil, he passed his examinations with distinction and was given a gold medal. The director of the Institute urged Kropotkin to give Kruglov his freedom to let him study at the university (where serfs were not admitted).

"He is sure to become a remarkable man, perhaps one of the glories of Russia; it will be an honour for you to have recognized his talents and to have given such a man to Russian science."

"I need him on my own estate", the prince replied to numerous applications made on the young man's behalf. On the estate there was nothing for Kruglov to do. After he had made a survey, he was ordered to sit in the servants' hall and wait at dinner. Kruglov's looks showed his disappointment. The princess (Kropotkin's second wife) thereafter took special pleasure in humiliating him. One day in the autumn she asked him to go and shut the entrance gate which a gust of wind had opened. "You have a porter for that", answered Kruglov, tried beyond endurance. For this action, he was placed under arrest and chained, to be sent away as a soldier.

A conversation between Peter Kropotkin and his father some time after the liberation of the serfs epitomizes the spirit of serfdom. "You must agree, father," said the younger man, "that you often punished your servants cruelly and without sufficient cause." The old prince did not deny the charge. "With these people", he replied, "it was impossible to do otherwise." Then, after a thoughtful pause, he continued :

"But what. I did was hardly worth speaking of. Now, take Sablev for example : he looks so soft and talks so gently, but he was really terrible with his serfs. How many times did they plot to kill him ! I, at least, never took advantage of my maids. But that old devil Tonkov carried on in such a way that the peasant women were going to inflict a terrible punishment on him ... Good-bye; *bonne nuit* !"

One of the terrors of every male serf was the possibility that he might be made a soldier. The armies of Nicholas numbered just over a million in 1826; some twenty years later their numbers had increased by about four hundred thousand. There was then no conscription. When a levy of recruits was ordered, the landowners and administrators of state domains had each to supply a certain number of men (calculated at so many for every 1000 male souls). As a rule, the village communities kept a roll of potential recruits, and sometimes decided by lot who was to go. Even here, interference from the owner or his steward was not uncommon. The domestic serfs, on the other hand, were entirely at the mercy of their lord. If he was dissatisfied with one of them, he could send him to the recruiting-board (even when there was no levy) and get a recruiting receipt. Such a receipt had considerable money value, as it could be sold to anyone whose turn it was to become or to provide a soldier. It could also be kept by the owner against the next recruiting levy.

The giving away of domestic serfs as recruits was a very common occurrence. Kropotkin describes the situation. When it became known that one of the servants was to be sent to the recruiting-board, gloom spread over the household. The victim was placed under guard in the office to prevent him getting away. When the

allotted man was taken out under escort, all his fellow
servants surrounded him. He made a deep bow, asking
forgiveness from everyone for his offences. If his father
and mother lived in the same village, they came to see
him off. He would bow to the ground before them. His
mother and other female relatives would intone their
lamentations as at a burial and in the same words. Then
the victim would enter on his twenty-five years' service.

The recruit was torn from his family and his native
village. If he had children, they were taken away to a
military orphanage to be brought up as soldiers. His
wife—it would be truer to say his widow—was left to
her own devices. After three years, she was legally
allowed to remarry. His village knew him no more.

In the days of Nicholas conditions in the army were
hard and discipline was cruel :

"Blows from the officers, flogging with birch rods
and with sticks for the slightest fault, were normal
affairs. The cruelty that was displayed surpasses all
imagination. Even in the Cadet School, where only
sons of the aristocracy were educated, a thousand
blows with birch rods were sometimes administered,
in the presence of the whole School, for a cigarette—
the doctor standing by the tortured boy, ordering the
punishment to end only when he ascertained that
the pulse was about to stop beating. Whereupon the
bleeding victim was carried away unconscious to the
hospital."

Even this was gentle compared to the punishment
meted out to common soldiers :

"When one of them appeared before a Court Martial, the sentence was that a thousand men should be
placed in two ranks facing each other, every soldier
armed with a stick of the thickness of a little finger
. . . and that the condemned man should be dragged
three, four, five and even seven times between these

two rows, each soldier administering a blow. Sergeants followed to see that full force was used. After one or two thousand blows the victim, spitting blood, was taken to hospital and attended to, in order that the punishment might be completed when he had more or less recovered from the first part of it. If he died under the torture, the execution of the sentence was completed upon the corpse."

Tsar Nicholas and his brother Michael knew no pity. No sentence was ever lightened. General Timofeev, a heartless martinet but a great favourite of the Emperor, would order a soldier to be flogged almost to death for a mistake made during a parade.

Any soldier who survived his service found a hard lot awaiting him at the end. He had lost his place in the village. His wife had remarried years before. His children had disappeared into the 'cantonist schools'. He had learnt no trade and had little inclination to work. He became a tramp or a beggar. Moltke, hardly a sentimentalist, was moved during a visit to Russia at the sight of a Crimean veteran begging outside the Kremlin :

"There stood the man who but a few short months ago had shed his blood for his country. Now he was begging outside the Kremlin, in the very heart of the empire which has grown great, exists and will continue to exist thanks to its faithful, pious, brave and neglected soldiers."

After serfdom and the army, officialdom formed the third great pillar of unreformed Russian society. The number of officials (*chinovniks*) exceeded half a million. Their name, for the Russian public, was synonymous with extortion and corruption. A Russian nobleman, in a memorandum submitted to Alexander II shortly after his accession, declared :

"All power is centred in the hands of the *chinovniks*. Casting a glance at the middle and lower spheres of the official world, we see a savage and greedy horde which has taken possession of Russia and enjoys without inhibition the rights of conquerors. It plunders all classes of people, robs the Imperial Treasury. . . . Having bound the hands of Ministers by centralization, paper formalism and countless signatures, having freed itself in this manner from every inspection and verification on the part of the central government, being everywhere the persecutor of freedom of expression which is . . . so much feared by thieves and plunderers, this Tartar horde, yclept Bureaucracy, robs and bullies Russia, producing a general discontent."

Corruption was especially prevalent in certain branches of the administration. The Ministry of Communications enjoyed a particularly unsavoury reputation. It had become, under the Minister Kleinmichel, "a veritable abyss of corruption and abuses, which swallowed up immense sums without the slightest advantage to the Empire". A typical piece of ingenious fraud is described by the Swedish Minister at St. Petersburg. Some years after the accession of Alexander II the astronomer Struve, when carrying out trigonometrical surveys outside St. Petersburg, adopted as his base one of the main roads leading to the capital. Struck by the curious nature of his results, he decided to measure his base, duly equipped with milestones registering the distances. Much to his surprise he discovered that each of the alleged miles was short by several yards. On measuring further roads, Struve made the same discovery. The roads had been constructed under Count Kleinmichel's régime. In fact, every department of the administration connected with construction or supplies was riddled with corruption. During the Crimean War, the military supply departments—at the soldiers' expense—were 'dishonoured by plundering such as history will shudder at'. The officials of the special Exchequer Courts in each province were profitably employed. Annual gifts from the district cashiers, the brandy farmers, and local contractors helped to keep them in funds. Their most lucrative operation, however, was recruiting, which, in official slang, they referred to as their *harvest*. Their methods were simple and effective.

In more exalted spheres transactions, if more refined in form, were hardly different in spirit. Count Vladimir Adlerberg I, Minister of the Imperial Household and all-powerful favourite of Nicholas I, kept a mistress, a lady married to a minor official. *Madame de* Bourkov, once a simple Latvian servant-girl, had made a career for herself, and was now, under a different name, a partner in a St. Petersburg fashion shop. People who desired a favour from the Court were well advised to pay a visit to the shop. There they might acquire a pair of gloves, at a grossly excessive price, after which their petitions were more likely to be successful.

Corruption shaded imperceptibly into the crudest forms of extortion. This was the chosen field of the rural police. Its victims were to be found more particularly among the religious minorities subject to special restrictions. They included Jews, Mohammedan Tartars and Bashkirs, sectarians, and, above all, the primitive Finnish tribes of north-eastern Russia and the miserable natives of Siberia. The Finnish tribes, 'poor, timid, stupid people', formed a regular gold-mine for the Russian officials. Inspectors of police and others would pay the Governor (the highest official in each Province) double the usual sum to be appointed to a district inhabited by Finns. The reason is easy to see :

"If the land-surveyor is travelling on business and passes a native village, he never fails to stop there. He takes the theodolite off his cart, drives in a post and pulls out his chain. In an hour, the whole village is in a ferment. . . . The elder come to pay their respects: the surveyor goes on measuring and making notes. They ask him not to cheat them out of their land, and he demands twenty or thirty roubles. They are glad to give it and collect the money; and he drives on to the next village of natives."

If the police found a dead body, they dragged it around for a fortnight—the frost made this possible—through the Finnish villages. In each village they declared that they had just found the corpse and meant to start an inquest. The people, to escape the inquest, paid the blackmail demanded of them. With Russian peasants, on the other hand, there were limits to what could be achieved.

The law courts of unreformed Russia took their general character from the rest of the administration. They were staffed by *chinovniks* and shared all the faults of the executive branch of government. In addition, they had distinctive shortcomings of their own. Proceedings were secret and in writing. Since a single civil suit could—in certain circumstances—pass through eleven courts, and since delays were profitable to the officials, law-suits dragged on for years. The judges enjoyed neither independence nor respect.

In practice, for the mass of the Russian people, the law did not exist. It was the upper classes and foreigners who were its principal victims. The latter, in particular, might have to choose between the hazards of the 'courts' and submission to frauds of the grossest kind. The state of the 'courts' and the near impossibility of enforcing the payment of debts was an important factor in retarding Russia's economic development.

The general condition of the Russian administration requires some accounting for. Officials in the lower ranges received a remuneration so miserable that they could not live on their pay alone. The poverty of *chinovniks* who had the folly to be honest, or were inexpert at gathering in their 'harvest', is illustrated by the two clerks in a provincial office who, during the wet season, reported for duty only on alternate days—they possessed only one pair of boots between them. Such poverty, combined with deplorable moral and educational standards, inevitably turned men into bribe-takers. In fact, corruption was considered scarcely reprehensible; it was taken for granted in all official circles.

Every form of administrative iniquity and abuse, moreover, was carefully protected by the absence of legal responsibility and by administrative secrecy. No official could be prosecuted without his superior's permission. Since the plunder was shared among all ranks of the administrative hierarchy, such permission was rarely granted. An official who was able to 'stimulate' the goodwill of his superiors was immune from prosecution. There was no control by the Russian public over the conduct of officials since the assemblies of nobles, established by Catherine the Great, dealt almost exclusively with the affairs of the nobility. The most effective protection of officialdom, however, lay in the secrecy of administrative action. No budget was published, and the entire financial administration was thus shielded from the public gaze. Judicial proceedings took place in secrecy. Discussion of administrative abuses was permitted only in the purely literary form of a work like Gogol's 'Government Inspector'. The censorship prevented any discussion of the conduct of individual officials. Not till the refugee Alexander Herzen published his *The Bell* (*Kolokol*) in London were specific abuses exposed. In these circumstances, officialdom enjoyed almost complete immunity. Infrequent inspections organized by the Senate (the highest judicial body of the empire) may have had some effect in the localities under review, but could not alter the general spirit of the administration.

The evident defects of this vaguely oriental system of administration had been aggravated by Nicholas I's heavy-handed paternalism.[1] Brought up and trained as a soldier, the Emperor became a fanatical devotee of uniformity, obedience, and discipline. Civilian officials and even students were put into uniform. Everything in the empire was arranged according to the principle of hierarchical subordination. Steeped in the military tradition, Nicholas liked to refer to his vast empire as his 'command'. A military spirit pervaded the administration. Members of the Tsar's military establishment, aides-de-camp who had distinguished themselves on the parade ground and whom he knew personally, were promoted to the highest offices of state. The inevitable outcome of this development had been further to undermine the spirit of legality in Russian public life.

The most typical institution of Nicholas's régime was the 'Third Division of His Majesty's Own Chancery', the all-powerful security police commonly known as the 'Third Division'. The activities of this body—created after the Decembrist Rising of 1825—were ubiquitous. According to its historian, "there was no aspect of Russian life that would escape its control". The government, it was felt, "had to know what was going on among the people, what were their thoughts, what they talked about, what occupied them; it became necessary to penetrate into men's hearts and most secret thoughts". Moreover, not content with spying and prying, the Third Division frequently "assumed judicial functions and determined the guilt of persons in matters which had nothing to do with public safety". The state police was, in fact, a state within the state. Its Director was a member of the Committee of Ministers; indeed, his position at times resembled that of a Prime Minister.

[1] In the description of Nicholas I's system of government use has been made of the excellent account in the second volume of Michael Florinsky's *Russia: A History and an Interpretation* (New York, 1953).

Two successive heads of the Division had been amongst the closest intimates of the Tsar.

After the Polish insurrection of 1830-1, the heavy hand of Russian repression had fallen both on the Congress Kingdom (the autonomous state set up by the Treaty of Vienna, of which the Tsar was the ruler) and on Russia's western provinces (the territories acquired in the partitions of the eighteenth century, where the landowning gentry was mainly of Polish nationality). In both areas together, some 5,000 estates were confiscated. It is estimated that roughly one-tenth of all noble estates in the Congress Kingdom were involved. Some 30,000 families of Polish noblemen from the western provinces were deported to the Caucasus, Siberia, and the lands beyond the Volga (officially, this policy was termed 'resettlement'). In Warsaw, Field-Marshal Paskievich, who ruled the Congress Kingdom from 1832 until his death in 1856, carried out a policy of ruthless Russification and suppression of Polish autonomy. In the Kingdom and the western provinces alike, no effort was spared to suppress Polish cultural life. There were heavy reprisals against the Catholic Church. Severe (and successful) pressure was brought to bear on the Uniats (who preserved the Greek-Orthodox ritual whilst recognizing the authority of the Pope) to rejoin the Orthodox Church. The Polish universities of Warsaw and Vilna were closed. Instruction in Polish secondary schools in the Kingdom had to be conducted in Russian. Any mention of even the most celebrated Polish writers was prevented by the censorship.

It was not Polish intellectual life alone that had suffered from the repression following the revolutions of 1830. In Russia also, Count Uvarov, as Minister of Education (1833-49), had introduced a system based on "the truly Russian, conservative principles of orthodoxy, autocracy and nationality, our last anchor of salvation and the best guarantees of Russia's strength and greatness". Uvarov had constructed his 'intellec-

tual dams' in the schools and universities of the empire;
the censorship and the Third Division saw to it that
writers and journalists conformed to the principles of
the official 'party line'.

The revolutions of 1848 removed the last vestiges of
intellectual freedom. In September 1849, even Uvarov
resigned because he was thought too liberal. His successor, the obscurantist Prince Shirinsky-Shikhmatov
immediately destroyed what little remained of university autonomy and academic freedom. Deans of Facul-
ties were ordered to supervise the contents of academic
teaching. Study of philosophy and of European constitutional law was discontinued, the teaching of logic
and psychology entrusted to professors of theology.

At the same time the censorship became still more
severe. Censors began to delete terms like 'forces of
nature' from text-books on physics and 'free currents of
air' from cookery books. (It was held that they might
have a political significance, and, indeed—faced with
the censorship terror—journalists and writers did resort to a variety of subterfuges.) The name of the great
writer Gogol could no longer be mentioned in print.
Almost every government department, down to the Post
Office and the Imperial Stud, could exercise ill-defined
functions of censorship over matters concerning its own
province. It could happen that an article written by a
high official of the Ministry of the Interior was banned
by the censor at the request of the Ministry of Education. A censor declared that "if one were to count all
officials in charge of censorship, their numbers would
greatly exceed that of books published every year".

Intensification of the censorship was accompanied by
a determined attempt to keep Russians from 'conta-
gious' contact with the West. Passports for foreign
travel became practically unobtainable. Study at
foreign universities, so common in an earlier age, was
no longer to be thought of. Nicholas's 'Iron Curtain'

was almost as effective as that erected by his latter-day successors.

It was under these conditions that in 1853 the Russian government blundered almost unwittingly and ill-prepared into war with England and France. Nicholas's elaborate diplomatic system produced in the hour of need no friends but many enemies. Still worse, owing in part to Russian backwardness, lack of railways and administrative inefficiency and corruption, still more to a faulty strategy,[1] the Russian armies on which all the care of the régime had been lavished, did not justify the high hopes of the Russian public. It was this that gave the death-blow to Nicholas's system of government. Many members of the upper classes had acquiesced in that system—however reluctantly—because it had raised Russian prestige in Europe. Now it was revealed that the military colossus stood on feet of clay. Of a peace-time army of around one million and a quarter only 350,000 could, after heroic exertions, be brought to the field of battle. The heavy sacrifices made for the army had been in vain : the system of Nicholas stood condemned.

The Tsar himself understood the extent of his failure. The last months of his life were darkened by a realization that his life's work lay in ruins. On March 2, 1855, the 'Iron Autocrat' died broken-hearted; rumour even spoke of suicide, and it is certain that he had of set purpose neglected an attack of influenza from which he was suffering. With the death of Nicholas, a pillar of the old régime came crashing to the ground.

[1] Strategically the defence of the Crimea was a costly blunder. Could the ill-organized allies have invaded the interior? What, in such an event, would have been the outcome of the conflict?

## Chapter Two

# The New Emperor

ALEXANDER, son of Nicholas, the new Emperor of
All the Russias, was born in Moscow on April 29
(April 17 o.s.), 1818. His mother, Alexandra Feodorovna
(before her baptism into the Orthodox religion she had
been Princess Charlotte of Prussia) was the daughter of
Frederick William III of Prussia and Queen Louise.
The later Frederick William IV and William I were her
brothers. Until her death in 1860, she maintained the
closest ties with her family in Berlin. Young Alexander,
almost 'with his mother's milk' imbibed a strong affection for Prussia and things Prussian which remained
with him throughout his later life. In 1829, at the age
of eleven, he paid his first visit to Berlin. His grandfather had appointed him colonel-in-chief of the Third
Prussian Uhlan Regiment. The child, until the end of
the visit, refused to appear in anything but his new
Prussian uniform. It was the beginning of a life-long
association with the Prusso-German army.

Alexander's early education bore a dual aspect. From
the tender age of six, as befitted a son of Nicholas, he
received a military training composed of drills and
parades. From 1829 onwards he attended the annual
cadet camps organized under his father's personal
supervision. Even his Christmas presents were of a
martial nature. Thus in 1831, his loving parents gave
him a bust of Peter the Great, a rifle, a sword, a box of
pistols, a parade uniform, and a set of china cups and
saucers depicting Russian soldiers of different arms.
However, whilst the young prince found pleasure in

29

parades and reviews, he showed little interest in the more serious aspects of military science. In the autumn of 1832, the Tsar complained of this to Captain Merder, his military tutor, and himself drew up a syllabus for the study of fortifications and gunnery; Alexander, reluctantly, had to apply himself to these subjects. In fact, he never acquired the slightest interest in scientific soldiering; throughout his life he remained a passionate addict of the parade-ground and the military review.

Nor did the civilian side of his education produce the desired results. The civilian tutor of the Tsarevich— and it is impossible not to recognize in the choice the hand of the Empress—was the romantic, 'liberal', and humanitarian poet Zhukovsky. When, in 1826, the tutor-elect submitted a detailed programme for the future development of his charge, he declared that its overall purpose was to be 'education for virtue'. Early in 1828, this education was begun in earnest. Soon the tutor had to remonstrate against excessive parades. In July, after Alexander had passed his first examination, Zhukovsky declared himself satisfied with the result; yet through his report runs an undertone of anxiety about his pupil's lack of diligence. Merder, in his diary, recorded the opinion he had formed of Alexander's character. The prince had a natural inclination to what was good. He had, however, a disposition to vagueness and hesitation when faced with obstacles or difficulties. The rest of Alexander's life would confirm the accuracy of the observation. The following year, Zhukovsky in his turn complained once again of the Tsarevich's lack of application. Alexander did not like lessons but preferred to play and roam about in the open air. In fact, he would never feel attracted to reading or study, whilst the desire for the open air foreshadowed a life-long passion for the chase. In 1831, there were further laments about apathy in the face of difficulties. Other defects made their appearance. Merder told Nicholas of his son's arrogance, disobedience, and quarrelsome disposition. Later in life Alexander on occasions showed himself to be extremely vindictive.

At the same time the child displayed a certain emotional sensibility and good nature which also would not be lacking in the later Tsar. During a walk with Merder along a St. Petersburg canal, Alexander (just thirteen years of age) noticed on one of the barges moored to the quay an old workman covered with a dirty mat, shaking and groaning. The child rushed across a plank, bent over the old man and asked him questions. When Merder, disapproving, followed Alexander on to the barge, he saw the boy wiping away the old man's tears with his handkerchief. Merder took a gold piece from his purse and gave it to Alexander—who left the coin on the old man's chest.

When, during the autumn of 1832, Merder developed heart attacks—not entirely unconnected with his pupil's wilfulness—Alexander at once changed his behaviour. He visited his invalid tutor regularly. When Merder had to go abroad for his health, Alexander used to write to him every Saturday. When he died in Rome in the spring of 1834, the Tsarevich wept bitterly. Throughout his life, Alexander was apt to burst into tears on formal or moving occasions.

Emotional outbursts were coupled with a certain good sense—already noted by Merder—which rarely left Alexander in later life.

In the spring of 1837, Alexander's formal education was declared to be complete. In spite of his lack of application, the future Emperor had acquired a good knowledge of Russian, French, German, Polish, and English. He had listened to lectures from Speransky, Russia's most distinguished statesman and jurist, on the laws of the Russian Empire. However, in spite of every effort, the Tsarevich had remained obstinately 'non-intellectual'. The future glories of his reign in the realms of literature and music left him cold and

unappreciative. Neither the Romanov nor the Hohen-
zollern strain was literary or artistic.

The completion of Alexander's formal education was
followed by a tour of the Russian Empire extending over
seven months. The Tsarevich was accompanied, among
others, by Zhukovsky, who spared no pains to influence
his pupil in the direction of pity and humanity. Although almost drowned in official reviews and receptions, the Tsarevich found time to visit the huts of the
peasants. He heard their complaints, he saw their
wretchedness. Again, during his visit to western Siberia
(the first ever paid by a Romanov), Alexander met some
of the exiled Decembrists (the military conspirators
against Nicholas I in 1825) and addressed them with
kindliness. Encouraged by Zhukovsky, he sent a special
messenger to his stern father asking for an alleviation of
their lot. Great was his joy—and even more that of the
good Zhukovsky—when Nicholas sanctioned a real improvement in the conditions of their exile. In remote
Viatka, amidst the forests of north-eastern Russia,
Alexander met a more recent exile—young Alexander
Herzen. At the instigation of Zhukovsky, the prince
asked his father to permit Herzen's return to St. Petersburg. Nicholas replied that this would be unfair to the
other exiles, but permitted an improvement in Herzen's
condition (exile in a town nearer Moscow). Herzen has
left a portrait of his youthful benefactor. The young
prince, he noted, had not his father's stern expression.
His features suggested rather good nature and indolence. Although barely twenty, he was already growing
stout. The few words he addressed to Herzen were
friendly, and he had not "the hoarse, abrupt, utterance
of his uncle Constantine".

The educational value of Alexander's tour was
limited. In the course of seven short months, he had to
visit no fewer than thirty provinces. Official engagements occupied most of his time. Yet the Tsarevich
gained impressions of lasting value. He wrote to one of

his tutors: "With my own eyes . . . I have seen our mother Russia, and I have learnt to love and respect her even more. Yes, we may be proud that we belong to Russia and call her our motherland." His genuine patriotism was a marked characteristic of the later emperor. Alexander's travels in Russia were followed by a grand tour of Europe to crown his official education. Again, as in his tour of Russia, the educational effects, to Zhukovsky's grief, were reduced by an excess of official engagements. During the tour (at Ems in 1839) the Marquis de Custine had an opportunity of twice getting a close view of the heir to the Russian throne. Custine noted that Alexander was stout for his age. Also that he had a melodious voice, which was unusual for his family. The expression of his face was gentle and well-meaning. However, the contrast between the youthful, smiling eyes and the constant contraction of the mouth appeared to suggest a lack of frankness and perhaps some hidden grief. His movements were graceful and noble; his manner was modest but without timidity. Truly the model of a prince, the French observer exclaimed with admiration. A second scrutiny, however, produced a less favourable impression. The prince's grace and noble bearing were indeed undeniable, but his face, in spite of its youth, now appeared inferior to his figure. The complexion was no longer fresh. The eyes betrayed a melancholy beyond his years. The face was round, Germanic rather than Slav, but the Greek profile recalled classical cameos. Custine noted a power of dissimulation frightening in one so young. (Was he remembering, consciously or unconsciously, the personality of the prince's uncle, Tsar Alexander I?) Above all, Custine again noted that the Tsarevich appeared to be suffering.

This last observation—although he hardly knew it—did credit to the Frenchman's perspicacity. Alexander, at this moment, was under a violent emotional strain : he was desperately in love with little expectation of a happy outcome. To find for him a suitable wife had been one of the principal objects of the Grand Tour. When the subject had first been mooted, the Tsarevich, then under the influence of the charms of a ballerina, had shown complete indifference. However, on passing through Darmstadt, he had fallen violently in love with the Princess Mary, the Duke's young daughter, then barely fifteen years of age. At once he had told his aides : "She is the woman of my dreams. I will never marry anyone but her." He had written forthwith to his parents (who had expected to find their future daughter-in-law at the court of Karlsruhe), asking permission to marry Mary. In reply, he had been told to hasten his return to St. Petersburg, where the matter would be discussed. Alexander, impatient and disappointed, confided to a member of his suite that, rather than renounce Mary, he would give up the throne. He had no wish to reign. He only wanted to find a worthy wife to grace his hearth and give him the highest happiness on earth— that of a husband and father.

Back in St. Petersburg, Alexander told his parents of his resolve. Nicholas demurred and, in the face of his son's impetuosity, gave the reason for his objection. Mary's father, Grand Duke Louis II of Hesse-Darmstadt, after two years of married life and the birth of two sons, had decided to end conjugal relations with his wife. Duke and Duchess had begun to live apart. The Duchess had led her own life and was credited with numerous frailties. In the spring of 1823, some fourteen years after these events, the court of Darmstadt learnt with amazement that she was pregnant. In July, a son was born.[1] Louis II, to avoid a scandal, assumed the paternity of the child. Everyone knew the true father, a man of such inferior station that nobody dared to name him. The following year the Duchess was delivered of another child by the same father : the Prin-

[1] Prince Alexander of Hesse, ancestor of the Battenberg (Mountbatten) family.

cess Mary. Alexander declared that this revelation made no difference to his determination that he would abandon the succession rather than live without Mary. Reluctantly Nicholas yielded. In the spring of 1840, the couple were formally betrothed. In December, Mary was received into the Orthodox Church as Maria Alexandrovna. In the following spring, Alexander and Mary were married with the traditional pomp and ceremonial appropriate to the occasion. The Tsarevich had shown that he could be stubborn when he meant to get his way.

There followed years of idyllic family happiness. A first child, a girl, died soon after birth, to the grief of the parents. But during the years which followed four sons and a daughter were born. Mary made a favourable impression on her new relations and on her future subjects. All agreed that she combined great beauty with perfect distinction. In spite of her youth, her tastes were of a serious kind. She devoted herself to charitable works, whilst her piety was the delight of the Holy Synod. The only fault the Court could find in her was some stiffness and formality of manner. Alexander—lavishing upon his wife consideration and affection—was enjoying the idyll which he had declared the object of his life's ambition.

Tsar Nicholas, however, would not allow his son to forget that he must one day be Emperor. Alexander was ordered to attend the meetings of the Council of Ministers. He was appointed Chancellor of Helsingfors University. Membership of other governmental bodies followed. In 1846, and again two years later, he presided over secret committees set up to study the problem of serfdom. In 1849, he succeeded an uncle as Colonel-in-Chief of all military schools and colleges. The Guards and Grenadier regiments were placed under his command. Moreover, Alexander now began to act as Regent during his father's (sometimes prolonged) absences from the capital. He became familiar with the personnel of the higher administration, civil as well as military. In fact, thanks to the care and forethought of his father, he was perhaps the best-prepared heir-apparent ever to ascend the Russian throne.

Introduced in this manner to the practical affairs of state, Alexander had become an increasingly convinced believer in his father's system of government. Scrupulously and with boundless veneration for his stern parent, he had carried out the different tasks assigned to him. Nicholas had rewarded this devotion with unlimited confidence. Alexander, under his influence, accepted the methods as well as the principles of the régime. In the committees on serfdom, he defended the interests of the landowning nobility. The revolutions of 1848 strengthened his conservative outlook. Yet his approach to the problems of government differed in some respects from that of Nicholas. The Swedish Minister at St. Petersburg noted that, if he had inherited his father's profound sense of duty, he understood that duty in a sense more consonant with the development of 'progressive' Russian thought and with the needs created by the advance of civilization.

Indeed, for all his repressive policies, even Nicholas I had been a consistent advocate of practical reforms and the removal of abuses. He described serfdom as a 'flagrant evil', and during his reign no fewer than nine secret committees wrestled with the problem of preparing its gradual abolition. Under the enlightened administration of P. D. Kisselev, the lot of the state peasants at least was considerably improved. Nicholas applauded Gogol's 'Government Inspector'. Throughout his reign he tried to bring some order into the jungle of the Russian legal system. During the early thirties, Speransky brought to a successful conclusion his great codification of the laws of the empire. Later, a committee under Bludov for years struggled with the problem of reforming the Russian courts. In fact, in bringing about far-reaching administrative and social reforms

Alexander was not departing from his father's system of government, but rather carrying forward his programme of reform to greater purpose.

In spite of his careful training, Alexander was reluctant to accept the overwhelming responsibility of imperial rule. Indeed, he once went so far as to express the wish not to survive his father, but fate willed it otherwise: on March 2, 1855, Nicholas I died, and Alexander Nicolaevich was Emperor of All the Russias. Shortly before the end, the dying emperor had addressed his son: "I hand over to you my command, but unfortunately not in such order as I should wish. I am leaving you many labours and anxieties." Alexander replied: "I hope that there [in Heaven] you will pray faithfully for your Russia and that I may receive assistance." "I shall faithfully do so", Nicholas answered. On the day after his accession, Alexander repeated this conversation to the members of the Imperial Council. "Reposing my trust in the prayer of my unforgettable father and in God's help, on which I have always relied and shall continue to do, I ascend the throne of my ancestors."

The accession of Alexander II was greeted by the Russian public with feelings composed in equal measure of uncertainty and hope. Some had heard rumours that he favoured the liberation of the serfs without land, others that he would faithfully protect the interests of the nobility. Many entertained hopes that a new reforming age was dawning. "A new era", wrote one of these, "has begun in our public affairs; may it also be a new era in the moral and social existence of every Russian." The Swedish Minister at St. Petersburg reported that, although for the present the government's attention was absorbed by the war, it was expected that, once peace was concluded, the new emperor would turn his attention to the urgent problems of domestic administration. Much was expected of him in this sphere. His excellent intentions were known.

Without possessing his father's eminent qualities, he yet had intelligence and a profound sense of duty. He understood this duty, moreover, in a more 'modern' sense than Nicholas had done.

Whatever the future might hold, however, the war had to be ended first. Since the beginning of February, allied attacks on Sevastopol had redoubled, and it was becoming doubtful whether the heroic defence could be continued much longer. Nicholas, before his death, had agreed to a meeting with allied representatives in neutral Vienna to discuss the terms of peace. Alexander now declared that he was ready to agree to the terms already accepted by his father. However, if the coming discussion did not offer the prospect of an honourable peace, he would "go bravely into battle at the head of his faithful Russia and the entire Russian people". In fact, the talks in Vienna ended without result : the allied representatives, who had agreed to terms not unacceptable to Russia, were disavowed by their governments.

Alexander was forced to stake everything on the defence of Sevastopol. When the French captured important sections of the city's fortifications, the Russian commander, Prince Michael Gorchakov, requested permission to evacuate the fortress. The Tsar would not hear of it. Should Sevastopol itself be overrun, the Crimea must be held at all costs. It was Nicholas's faulty strategy carried to the extreme. During June the position of the defenders surprisingly improved. Alexander called for offensive operations : Gorchakov, against his better judgment, carried out the unsuccessful attack on the Chernaya which cost the Russians 8,000 casualties. Three weeks later the allies opened a fierce bombardment in preparation for a general assault. Gorchakov, convinced that defence was hopeless, evacuated the city on the night of September 8–9. Its defence had cost the Russians more than 100,000 killed and wounded.

Undaunted, Alexander continued the struggle. His manifesto announcing the loss to the Russian people struck a defiant note. He admonished Gorchakov not to lose heart but to remember 1812 and trust in Providence. Sevastopol was not Moscow, the Crimea was not Russia. Two years after the fire of Moscow, the victorious Russian armies entered Paris. "We are the same Russians still, and God is with us." The banner of St. Sergius, which had been with Peter the Great at Poltava and with the Russian home guard in 1812, was dispatched to Gorchakov's headquarters in the Crimea. At a council of war in Moscow it was decided to hold the Crimea. Nicolaev at the mouth of the Bug (Russia's second naval arsenal) also must be placed in a state of defence. Alexander himself went to that town to supervise the work. He remained for six weeks, and before returning to St. Petersburg visited his troops outside Sevastopol. He returned to the capital encouraged by the spirit he had seen in his armies.

However, his principal advisers, led by Nesselrode, the aged Foreign Minister, felt the need for peace. It was known that neutral Austria and the allies had agreed on terms of peace to be submitted to Russia in the form of an ultimatum. Sweden had signed a treaty associating herself with the Western powers. The King of Prussia, Russia's only friend, sent word that he might be forced to join the allies. Complete isolation threatened Russia. Still Alexander was unwilling to yield. "We have", he wrote to Gorchakov, "reached the limit of concession compatible with Russian honour. I will never accept humiliating terms, certain that every true Russian feels as I do. All that is left for us, crossing ourselves, is to march straight ahead and defend by united effort our native land and national honour."

At the end of December, an Austrian envoy presented the terms concerted with England and France. Not only was Russia asked to consent to the neutralization of the Black Sea, but also to cede some territory in

Bessarabia to remove her from the navigable portion of the Danubian estuary. The terms were hard and, in the Tsar's opinion, dishonourable. Would he agree, even at this price, to end hostilities which no longer offered any hope of success?

When Alexander consulted his advisers, all agreed that Russia needed peace, but all were reluctant to accept the Austrian terms. It was decided to make counter-proposals, but the Austrian government remained firm. Unless its terms were accepted unconditionally, it would break off diplomatic relations. When the Tsar put the issue again to his Council, all present declared that peace was an absolute necessity. Nesselrode in particular feared that, by the following year, Russia might be faced with a general European coalition. She might be effectively blockaded and her economic future impaired. Sooner or later, she would be forced to make peace, and later on the terms might be still more onerous. Other speakers feared that the Crimea and the Caucasus, even Finland and Poland, might in the end be lost. A continuation of the war would lead to bankruptcy. If Russia continued hostilities, she might be reduced to the state of Sweden after the death of Charles XII. If she now accepted terms which did not impede her development, she would, within a few years, be as powerful as she had been before the war. A peace concluded at present, therefore, need only be a truce. Postponed by a year or two, it would leave the empire in a state of exhaustion from which it would take decades to recover. Unconditional acceptance of the Austrian terms, however unpalatable, was a necessity.

The final decision, however, rested with Alexander alone. Whilst deeply impressed with the prudence of the counsels he had received, he felt passionately, as a soldier, that acceptance of the ultimatum would be a shameful act. Russia was undefeated. She still had a numerous army; she had her historic memories, her patriotism, her powers of endurance. Her immense territory and severe climate opposed difficulties to any invader. She might follow the example of 1812 and await the enemy at home. Such were the views of Alexander's military entourage, of many patriotic ladies in the two capitals, and, in general, of people who had no official responsibility. Alexander was in sympathy with this view; its principal spokesman was his younger brother, Constantine. Indeed, after the meeting of the Council, a 'passionate discussion' between the two brothers took place in the apartments of the Empress-dowager. Alexander drew his brother's attention to the difficulties of the situation : Prussia threatened to join Russia's enemies; the losses in manpower were vast (Russia's total loss of life in the war has been estimated at around 600,000); the raising of new recruits was becoming more difficult; last, but not least, the country's financial resources were exhausted. With a heavy heart he had, therefore, decided to accept the Austrian terms. With a deep sense of his responsibility, Alexander took the first important decision of his reign.

On March 30 peace between Russia and her enemies was signed in Paris. Alexander announced the event to the Russian people in a manifesto which contained the first official promise of internal change. "With the help of divine Providence, which has always protected Russia's welfare . . . may her internal well-being be strengthened and perfected; may truth and mercy reign in her courts; and may there develop in all spheres the urge towards enlightenment and every form of useful activity. May everybody, under the protection of laws equally just for all and giving all equal protection, enjoy the fruits of his honest labour." It was a promise to the Russian public that the character of the administration would change.

Even before the signing of the peace, the government had already taken measures which showed that a new spirit was abroad. Within a month of his accession,

Alexander withdrew the vexatious restrictions against religious sects. The Minister of the Interior responsible for the persecution of the sectaries was dismissed. Warned about malversation in the Army's supply services, the Tsar ordered a strict inquiry. A foreign diplomat sympathetic to reform rejoiced at the dismissal of the Ministers of the Interior and Communications "as if we had gained two major victories over the enemy". Before the end of the year a more tolerant régime had been introduced for the Catholic Church in Poland. Restrictions on intellectual life were relaxed. Students were once more admitted to the universities without limitation; young scholars were again sent abroad at public expense; works prohibited by the censor could again appear in print. It was known, moreover, that the Tsar had ordered the complete overhaul of the censorship regulations. No one in Russia was left in doubt that a period of 'thaw' had begun.

The 'thaw' assumed impressive proportions with Alexander's coronation at Moscow in September 1856. Favours announced in the Coronation Manifesto went beyond what was usual on such occasions. Substantial concessions were made to the Tsar's poorest subjects : tax arrears amounting to forty million roubles were cancelled; regions severely hit by the war received tax exemptions; a juster distribution of the poll-tax was promised. All recruiting was suspended for three years. The institution of the cantonists[1] was abolished, and 80,000 children of soldiers were thus, at one stroke, returned to their families. Jews were relieved from special taxes. Restrictions imposed on Polish nobles in the western provinces were removed. There was a wide amnesty for political prisoners; the surviving Decembrists were allowed to return, as well as hundreds exiled in 1849. A concession greeted with delight by the upper

[1] These were the sons of men called up for military service who were compulsorily brought up as soldiers in military orphanages.

classes was the removal of the heavy passport fee imposed under Nicholas. The 'iron curtain' painstakingly erected by the last Tsar was being removed by his heir.

Another important development was being started. In October 1855, a committee had been set up to study foreign railway legislation. On the day the conclusion of peace became known in St. Petersburg, Alexander met Baron Stieglitz, Russia's foremost and wealthiest financier. "The peace is signed; we must profit by it", the Tsar remarked. Encouraged by the Tsar, Stieglitz journeyed to Paris to discuss railway finance with French banking interests. An agreement was reached between a consortium organized by Stieglitz (which included the Crédit Mobilier, Péreire and Fould of Paris, Hope of Amsterdam, and Baring of London) and the official Russian representatives led by Kleinmichel's successor, Chevkin. The new company was to construct five major lines, which would at the same time promote the export of Russian grain through the Baltic and Black Sea ports, and facilitate the movement of troops towards the south and west. The Russian government guaranteed a fixed rate of interest on the sums spent by the consortium, provided the cost of construction did not exceed a specified maximum per mile.

From the early measures of the new ruler, it might well appear that Russia was set on the road towards 'democratization' and internal development. However, it soon became apparent that the new Tsar was not only benevolent but also weak. Granville, Queen Victoria's special envoy at the coronation, considered him "well-intentioned but weak as water". He looked "intelligent and amiable", but did not give the impression of having much strength "either of intellect or of character". This weakness, which would have done little damage in a constitutional ruler, was a great liability in an autocratic one. A faction-fight at the very centre of power had begun almost at the moment of Alexander's accession. It weakened the authority of the government, reduced the popularity of the Tsar, and came close to plunging the empire into chaos.

Nicholas I in his day had been surrounded by a small closed clique of favourites—the Adlerbergs, Baranovs, Shuvalovs, and Orlovs. The less-favoured members of the Court nobility hoped, after the change of ruler, to deprive this camarilla of its exclusive enjoyment of imperial favours. However, Nicholas's circle had already succeeded in establishing its ascendancy over the heir-apparent. His accession was followed by new favours. Adlerberg Junior, Alexander's personal friend and companion (a good-natured gambler), was given a palace and an annual grant of 20,000 roubles for its maintenance. Baranov received a present of 300,000 roubles. Orlov sold back to the state for twice that sum a palace Nicholas had given him the previous year. Shuvalov obtained for his son Peter—a simple colonel aged thirty—the responsible position of Chief of Police in the capital, at a salary of 80,000 roubles. Petersburg was unfavourably impressed by the appointment of one so young and inexperienced.

The favours shown to members of the camarilla infuriated the Court nobility. In revenge, they now professed a desire for honesty in public affairs little in accord with Russian tradition. There was severe criticism of the depredations made on the public funds. The camarilla replied with an attempt to remove hostile influences from the Tsar's entourage. The most important of these was the Empress Mary. Even before Alexander's accession, the Empress had waged a bitter struggle to save her easy-going husband from the damaging influence of his companions. To do this, she had taken upon herself a share in the responsibilities of government. Every night, after retiring with the Emperor, she read to him important papers and discussed impending measures of the government. Indolent by nature and trusting her judgment, Alexander often listened to her advice. This did not suit the camarilla. It was insinuated that the Empress wished to germanize Russia; she was given the malicious nickname of 'bourgeoise allemande' (one is reminded of Marie Antoinette, 'l'Autrichienne'). Unfortunately for the Empress, these attacks coincided not only with a pregnancy (in the spring of 1857) but also with an attachment formed by Alexander for Princess Alexandrine Dolgoruky, one of her maids of honour. The camarilla created for the princess the position of an official mistress; kind 'friends' then exaggerated the affair to the Empress. On the advice of a confessor in league with the camarilla, she had the imprudence to reproach her husband with his infidelity. The result was an estrangement, even a temporary separation. The object of the camarilla was achieved.

To forget his domestic troubles, Alexander, now eager to avoid his wife's company, gave himself up to a life of dissipation in the company of his old friends. It was now that he first gave full rein to his lifelong passion for the chase, particularly bear-hunting. The Empress changed her tactics. She resolved—to regain some influence and restore some semblance of normal relations—to turn a blind eye to her husband's infidelity. She struck up an alliance with the other female members of the imperial family, especially the dowager-empress. Thanks to this, she was able to regain at least part of her former influence. She did much to confirm the Tsar in his resolution to liberate the serfs, and later played a fatal role as the protectress of the Pan-Slav movement.

Whilst at the centre of power intrigue succeeded intrigue, discontent was rapidly spreading among all classes of the population. There was unrest among the peasantry in the interior of the empire; the gentry felt alarm at the prospect of changes in the institution of serfdom; numerous officials had lost their posts in the interests of economy or as part of the campaign against corruption. Officers, especially in the favoured Guards

45

regiments, were irritated by frequent changes in uniforms and by alterations in military regulations. Many were threatened with premature retirement as a result of large cuts in the military forces. The small *rentiers* were hit by a reduction in the rate of interest paid by government savings-banks. (This had been intended, apart from economy, to divert capital into railway construction.)

People blamed the Emperor for their many and varied discontents. The British Minister at St. Petersburg reported that although Alexander was by universal consent "an amiable and well-intentioned man", everybody considered him a weak ruler. The complaints of his want of capacity and decision grew "daily louder and louder". Criticism of highly placed individuals and government measures was becoming widespread, especially in St. Petersburg. Officers in a fashionable restaurant put forth a drawing of a bear with the head of the Emperor and the words "he who goes a-hunting loses his job" ("*qui va à la chasse, perd sa place*"). In part, this orgy of criticism was the natural reaction to the iron rule of Nicholas, the inevitable consequence of a relaxation of the reins of government. However, the result of the ferment was to weaken the prestige and authority of the Emperor and his government. This would be felt severely the moment the government attempted to make changes more far-reaching than minor 'liberal' concessions. It would then appear that a well-meaning 'thaw' did not of necessity promote the more serious task of reform.

*Chapter Three*

# The Tsar Liberator

BEHIND the ferment caused by the great 'thaw' lurked Russia's basic social problem, the question of the future of serfdom. "The question of questions, the evil of evils", a high official confided to an acquaintance, "the first of all our misfortunes, is serfdom". All other evils of Russian life—and they were numerous—were connected with this cancer, and would lose much of their gravity by its removal. The question was not a new one : both Alexander I and Nicholas I had made half-hearted and unavailing attempts to pave the way for the abolition of serfdom. The opposition of the gentry and of most of the higher officials had frustrated their designs. Alexander II, from his experience as president of two secret committees, knew the difficulties of the task. Yet the policy of gradual liberation was a tradition which he had inherited from his father. Both shared the conviction that, sooner or later, serfdom would have to go. The experience of the Crimean War, moreover, had made clear to everyone that fundamental reforms at an early date could no longer be avoided if Russia was to retain her position among the powers.

Alexander's conversion to the necessity for abolition had been a gradual process. In the secret committees over which he presided he had, on the whole, defended the interests of the landowners. However, as he himself told Turgeniev, the latter's 'abolitionist' *Sportsman's Sketches* had left their mark on his impressionable mind. A general conviction of the need for reform combined with unrest among the peasant soldiers returned from the Crimea completed his conversion. Soon after his accession, rumours began to circulate that he favoured the abolition of serfdom. On April 11, 1856, he had made his first public pronouncement on the most important problem of his reign. He told representatives of the Moscow nobility : "For the contradiction of certain unfounded reports, I think it necessary to tell you that I do not at present intend to abolish serfdom; but certainly, as you well know yourselves, the existing manner of owning serfs cannot remain unchanged. It is better to abolish serfdom from above than to await the time when it will begin to abolish itself from below. I request you, gentlemen, to consider how this may be achieved, and to submit my words to the nobility for their consideration."

Shortly after his return to St. Petersburg, the Tsar consulted the Minister of the Interior about the best method of introducing a policy of 'gradual endeavours towards the liberation of the privately owned serfs'. The Minister, Lanskoy, recommended as a first step the preparation of a plan for liberation by stages. In consequence, he was asked to collect the relevant information from different ministries and to prepare a historical résumé on the evolution of serfdom and proposals made for its limitation since the time of Peter the Great. He was also told to use the coming coronation in Moscow for a private sounding of visiting marshals of nobility (the elected leaders of the local nobility in districts and provinces).

These preparatory measures reveal two aspects of Alexander's intentions at this stage. In the first place, he envisaged the abolition of serfdom by gradual stages rather than its immediate suppression. In addition, rather than bring about this emancipation by the action of the government alone, he hoped to obtain the cooperation of the Russian nobility. (Both these notions Alexander had inherited from his two immediate predecessors and their advisers.)

The first attempt to enlist the support of the nobility was a failure. The speech to the Moscow nobles, similar remarks to some marshals of nobility visiting St. Petersburg, repeated hints from Lanskoy to the marshals, produced not the slightest effect. The representatives of the nobility simply replied that they did not know on what principles the government intended to base its policy; they could not elicit those principles by themselves.

Alexander, therefore, decided that the first step must be taken by the government. In accordance with Russian administrative practice, he set up a secret committee under his own presidency. In his absence, it would be presided over by Orlov, the President of the Imperial Council. Orlov, then seventy-one years of age, was known as a convinced defender of serfdom. The majority of the committee was composed of officials hostile to abolition. Lanskoy alone, a Freemason who under Alexander I had sympathized with the Decembrists, was well-disposed. His only support was likely to come from Jacob Rostovtsev, one of the Tsar's adjutants-general.

Alexander himself opened the first meeting of the committee. He explained that several of his ancestors had tried, at various times, to improve the lot of the serfs. Their efforts had met with little success. Serfdom had now outlived its day and the time had come to consider "with due care and deliberation" arrangements which would lead to its eventual abolition. With regard to these, the resumé drawn up by the Ministry of the Interior raised a number of important questions. Was all the land, including that at present farmed by the serfs for their own use, to be considered the property of the landowners? If so, should there be legal recognition of the peasants' customary right of use? Again, should the owners be compensated for the loss of their serfs' services and such land as they might be asked to surrender? If so, to what extent should the burden of the operation be borne by the exchequer? It was for the committee to consider these questions and submit their recommendations.

Russian official procedure was slow and cumbersome, and the work of the committee was not advanced by the fact that there was profound disagreement amongst its members. The majority, led by Orlov, Adlerberg Senior, Gagarin, Panin (the influential Minister of Justice), and Muraviev (Minister of Imperial Domains), considered all reform to be both premature and dangerous. Their aim was to 'apply a brake', to prevent liberation, and, if unavoidable, to reduce its scope to an inescapable minimum. Lanskoy, the protagonist of emancipation, was supported only by some senior officials of his own Ministry. Without the backing of the Emperor, he had no hope of success.

While the committee was blocking all action, the Ministry of the Interior had worked out its own plan of emancipation. Lanskoy proposed that, for the time being, all land should remain the legal property of the landowner. The peasants should simply be protected in their customary right to form part of the estate. They should not pay for their *personal* freedom (the complete severance of *all* ties which bound them to their former owners). Their huts and farmyards (homesteads) would become their personal property, for which they would make payments to the owner spread over a period of ten to fifteen years. At the end of this 'period of transition', they would obtain full independence. In the intervening period, all necessary legal arrangements for the termination of serfdom would be made. Since all land remained in law the property of the squire, he would receive no compensation. The peasants would pay for the part of the estate allocated for their use either in money or in labour. No financial intervention by the government would be needed. The new system might be introduced gradually in the various provinces of the empire.

While this plan was in preparation, the Emperor had been abroad (summer of 1857). At Kissingen in Germany, he met Kisselev, who had been a warm protagonist of emancipation under Nicholas I. "I am more than ever determined", Alexander confided to his father's trusted adviser, "but have no one to help me in this important and pressing matter." Kisselev noted in his diary that the Tsar was clearly determined to carry through the emancipation but was meeting with difficulties on all sides.

On returning to Russia, Alexander discovered to his annoyance that the secret committee had made no progress whatever. He therefore appointed his brother Constantine, a radical reformer, a member of that body. Under his influence some headway was made. At this point matters were accelerated by an unexpected development. About the middle of November, Nazimov, the Governor-General of Lithuania (which embraced the provinces of Kovno, Grodno, and Vilna) arrived at St. Petersburg with a petition from the local nobility. The nobles of the three provinces requested permission to give *personal* freedom to their serfs while retaining possession of all the land. (Similar arrangements had already been introduced in the Baltic provinces under Alexander I.) The majority in the secret committee, to whom the matter was referred, supported the proposal. They hoped that it might pave the way for a general liberation without land throughout the empire.

The petition brought by Nazimov and its support by the secret committee impelled Alexander to his first decisive intervention in the liberation struggle. He declared categorically that the Lithuanian request for landless liberation must be rejected. Instead, the committee should take steps at once to draft legislation based on Lanskoy's proposals. After liberation, the peasants should receive their homesteads as their own property. They must retain the right to cultivate the land they were farming at present in return for a fixed rent in money or labour dues. Three meetings of the committee sufficed to formulate these principles. On December 2 (November 20 o.s.), Alexander signed the celebrated Rescript (an imperial order addressed to an individual, usually a high official) to Nazimov, containing his reply to the petition of the Lithuanian nobility. The Governor-General was instructed to form committees in each of the three provinces. These were to consist of the provincial marshal of nobility as president, one elected representative of the nobility for each district (the administrative sub-unit of the province), and two experienced landowners appointed by the Governor. Each committee should prepare a draft project of liberation based on the following principles: the landowners retained ownership of all the land; the peasants would, however, acquire their homesteads after payments spread over a fixed number of years; they would have the *use* of such land as was necessary for their subsistence and for the payment of taxes, for which right they would pay the owner in money or labour. Manorial jurisdiction would be preserved. When the work was completed, each committee would elect two delegates to a Commission for the whole of Lithuania, which would also include one experienced landowner from each province appointed by the Governor, and a representative of the Ministry of the Interior. The Commission would then bring together the three separate projects and submit to the Governor a plan for the whole of Lithuania. The latter would forward the plan to the Ministry of the Interior for submission to the Tsar.

The Imperial Rescript was accompanied by an instruction from Lanskoy to Nazimov. This stated clearly (as the Rescript had omitted to do) that after a twelve-year period of transition, it was intended to abolish serfdom. At the end of this period it would be illegal to sell serfs, to give them away, or to transplant them against their wishes. It would also become illegal to turn them into domestics. In fact, steps would be taken first to limit and finally to abolish the class of domestic serfs. If the landowners of Lithuania felt unable to accept these proposals, their objections must be stated in their final project.

Neither the Rescript nor Lanskoy's instruction was originally intended for publication. Yet only two days after signing the Rescript, Alexander communicated the content of these documents to the marshal of nobility of a central Russian province with the words: "I have decided to carry this matter to its conclusion and hope you will persuade your nobility to help me." Two days later, Lanskoy addressed a circular to the governors and marshals of nobility of all the provinces of European Russia. With it, he enclosed a copy of the Rescript and of his instructions to Nazimov—"for information and action should the nobility of your province express a similar desire". Thereafter, the matter no longer concerned the nobles of Lithuania alone but the whole of the Russian nobility. Would the rest of the nobles now take the initiative which Alexander desired?

The Tsar expected the nobles of his capital to take the lead. On December 21, he received a delegation come to thank him for his presence at a ball. Having thanked the marshal for his hospitality, he observed that their Governor-General (whilst ordinary provinces had simple Governors, those of special importance, or sometimes groups of provinces, were administered by Governors-General) had explained to them his wishes in the peasant question. It was his firm resolve that the matter should be settled. The principles laid down by him were oppressive to neither side. "I hope", the Tsar concluded, "that you will show a sincere interest in this matter, and will turn your attention to a class of people who deserve that their situation should be justly assured. Further delay is impossible; the matter must be dealt with now and not postponed to a distant future. That is my unshakable resolution." Turning to the

Governor-General, he added : "I ask you to co-operate with and lead the nobility; help them if there are difficulties." Thus were the Emperor's intentions revealed for the first time to the Russian public. Official publication of the Rescript to Nazimov followed. A decisive step had been taken; to stop now would be virtually impossible.

In any case, nothing was further from the Emperor's mind. On January 20, 1858, the hitherto secret committee on peasant matters became officially the "Main Committee on the Peasant Question for the Review of Projects and Suggestions concerning the Peasantry", known more briefly as the Main Committee. By the end of the year, forty-four provincial committees and two covering a group of provinces were wrestling with their draft projects for liberation. The policy embodied in the Rescript to Nazimov which was now being carried out marked Alexander's third approach to the problem. His speech at Moscow in the spring of 1856 had been part of an unavailing attempt to prod the nobility into taking the initiative. The setting up of the secret committee had ushered in an unsuccessful effort to draft a peasant statute with the help of officials in St. Petersburg. Now the Tsar was trying to achieve better results by combining direction from the centre with local initiative. The new approach contained two novel features. For the first time in Russian history, a Tsar had appealed to the entire nobility of the empire to co-operate in a major legislative enactment. Moreover, by the publication of the Rescript, he had for the first time submitted a burning question to the general Russian public. Both the nobility, therefore, and the intelligentsia (students, journalists, doctors, and members of professional groups in general) now entered the lists as champions or opponents of emancipation. The future of serfdom had become the issue of the day.

The announcement that the Tsar intended to liberate the serfs split the whole of Russian society into two groups, the abolitionists and the 'planters'—by which name the opponents of liberation soon came to be known, thanks in no small part to the journalistic genius of Alexander Herzen, the revolutionary socialist in exile. The 'abolitionists', writers, journalists, and university professors with a sprinkling of merchants and liberal officials, at once began a public campaign to demonstrate their support for the Tsar. In January 1858, a great banquet at the Moscow Merchants' Club was addressed by a succession of distinguished professors and publicists representing every shade of Russian opinion. When the well-known editor Michael Katkov proposed the health of the Tsar, he was greeted with prolonged cheers. The loudest applause of all, however, was reserved for Kokorev, the self-made millionaire spokesman of the Moscow merchants.[1] Kokorev appealed to his fellow merchants to subscribe to a great redemption fund to help the peasants pay the landowners for their homesteads and such land as they might receive after liberation. All the merchants, he declared with truth, were descended from the peasantry. They all—and particularly the farmers of spirits,[2] of whom he himself was one—owed their wealth to money paid by peasants. What an opportunity to show their gratitude today! The banquet was followed by others organized by Kokorev at which enthusiastic speeches by scholars and literary men were followed by ovations before the portrait of the Tsar.

The Russian press, which had received permission at last to discuss the peasant problem, shared in the

[1] This is how Kokorev was described by a Swedish diplomat: ". . . a spirit farmer, who by this trade as well as by other more or less legal methods, has acquired an immense fortune. . . . There is not a single industrial enterprise of any importance which does not number him among its founders; not a single well-written article in an economic journal of which he is not the author. He is the hero of Russia's rising industry."
[2] The sale of *vodka* was a state monopoly farmed out to merchant-entrepreneurs, who frequently made large fortunes.

abolitionist enthusiasm. In its issue of February 15, Herzen's *Kolokol* (published in London but with a considerable circulation inside Russia) carried the famous article 'After Three Years', which began and ended with the words 'Thou hast conquered, O Galilean!' Chernyshevsky, another radical journalist, compared the task undertaken by Alexander to that of Peter the Great. Young Peter Kropotkin, then a student in the Cadet School, later recalled how "all intellectual St. Petersburg was with Herzen, and particularly with Chernyshevsky. . . . I remember how the officers of the Horse Guards, whom I saw every Sunday after church-parade at the home of my cousin, used to side with Chernyshevsky, the leader of the advanced party in the emancipation struggle. The whole disposition of St. Petersburg, whether in the drawing-rooms or in the streets, was such that it was impossible to go back."

More directly useful to the Tsar than the enthusiastic but rather ineffectual support of the intelligentsia and the merchants was the assistance and encouragement of two other groups. Of these, the first consisted of a handful of reformers in the government itself. Lanskoy, the Minister of the Interior, had from the start been the driving force behind the policy of liberation. He, in his turn, leant heavily on his two younger and more energetic assistants, Soloviev and Nicholas Miliutin. The latter in particular—owing to his enthusiasm and technical knowledge—had soon become a leading figure in the abolitionist ranks. Another prominent supporter of emancipation was Alexander Gorchakov, the diplomat who, shortly after the Crimean War, had become Minister of Foreign Affairs. A school-fellow of the poet Pushkin, brought up in the 'liberal' atmosphere of Alexander I's early years, he was a reformer by personal inclination. In addition, his desire for a political *rapprochement* with France militated in the same direction. Early in 1858 a foreign observer recorded that Gorchakov "still wished to move forward like a student"

*Fem. influence in politics*

and spoke of nothing but 'progress'. Another foreign
diplomat at the end of 1859 went so far as to speak of
"the omnipotent influence which Prince Gorchakov has
enjoyed these last three years". His was a powerful influence on the side of the abolitionists.

More important even than these official influences—
which were, after all, more than counter-balanced in
the official sphere by the Orlovs, Panins, and Muravievs
—was the existence of prominent abolitionists in the
Tsar's immediate entourage. The Empress Mary, who,
by resigning herself to her husband's infidelities had re-
gained much of her influence, was a warm supporter of
the abolitionist cause. So, curiously enough, was Alexandrine Dolgoruky, the mistress who had supplanted her
in Alexander's affection. (She is the heroine of *Smoke*,
one of Ivan Turgeniev's novels.) The third in this tri-
umvirate of feminine influences (and this was characteristic of Alexander) was the Tsar's aunt by marriage,
the Grand-Duchess Helen (a former Württemberg princess). A woman of wide cultural interests, her musical
and literary *soirées* had become the meeting place of
all that was cultured and enlightened in St. Petersburg
society. Her interests, however, were not confined to
culture. She aspired to a political role, and, at two important junctures her influence over her nephew was
considerable. The first of these was during the liberation
struggle. It was in her salon that Alexander met the
leading abolitionists, Miliutin, Samarin, Cherkassky. It
was she who provided him with much of the information he needed to carry out his task. Moreover, her
assistance proved invaluable to another abolitionist
member of the imperial family, the Grand-Duke Constantine. Alexander's younger brother was a reformer
heart and soul; with an enthusiasm which usually out-
ran discretion, he had thrown himself into the struggle
against the powerful 'planters'.

The opponents of liberation formed a powerful
phalanx composed of two distinct elements. They were

led by a group of influential Ministers, headed by Orlov and Panin. The former, late in 1857, was described by a shrewd observer as 'still the first man of the empire' and 'the soul of the government'. Panin, the other 'planters'' leader, was described as a *"grand seigneur in the fullest sense of the term; un homme d'autrefois* immutable in his principles". When he came to realize that he could no longer please his sovereign, he retired rather than, as he himself said, "bow his grey head before the idol of progress".

Orlov, Panin, and their supporters in governmental spheres knew that liberation would mean the end of the existing social order and were determined to fight it to the end. They attempted—not without some success—to frighten the Tsar with the spectre of a peasant rising which, they claimed, would inevitably follow the abolition of serfdom. If these were the generals, their army consisted of the great majority of the provincial gentry resolved to fight for its land and its privileges. On every one of the provincial committees set up to prepare the projects of emancipation, the 'planters' formed the majority. Only an enlightened minority, varying in size, was prepared to apply conscientiously the principles laid down by Lanskoy on the Tsar's behalf. The majorities had no thought but opposition or obstruction. In effect, therefore, the 'planters' controlled both the Main Committee and all the provincial committees. It looked doubtful whether, in the face of their opposition, it would prove possible to apply the policy of the Rescript.

In fact, by the spring of 1858 matters were once again grinding to a standstill. The immediate problem was to establish a measure of uniformity in the proceedings of the many provincial committees. This was the first time in Russian history that locally elected bodies had been called upon to discuss matters of such vital importance. Moreover, it was clear that they were discussing the problem in a spirit at variance with the intentions of the government. The indefatigable Ministry of the Interior proposed to issue new directives. A draft instruction laid down that the object of the emancipation was the complete independence of the peasants from their former masters and their endowment with land. This draft, submitted by Lanskoy to the Main Committee, was duly rejected by that body. The Tsar, through his confidant Rostovtsev, ordered the issue of a new directive which paid more attention to the hereditary rights of the nobility. Under Rostovtsev's influence, the principles of the draft were modified. It was now declared the object of imperial policy that the serfs should become personally free and enjoy the hereditary use of their huts and farmyards. The redemption of these would be voluntary within a period to be laid down. The question of land allotments for the liberated serfs was passed over in silence. The new programme readily won the support of the Main Committee. It was confirmed by the Tsar and transmitted by Lanskoy to the provincial committees for their guidance. The Ministry of the Interior had suffered a major defeat at the hands of the 'planter' majority.

Moreover, the new circular coincided with the decision of the government to restrict the unfettered discussion of emancipation. The publication of the Rescript to Nazimov had been followed by a lively press discussion. Censorship had been lenient, and extreme as well as moderate views had found expression. Amongst those who dvocated radical solutions was Professor Kavelin, the Tsarevich's tutor in Russian law, who had published two articles on the subject. His analysis of relations between the government, the landowners, and the serfs had led to three drastic conclusions. The existing legal relationship between owners and peasants must be terminated, since for a long time to come no Russian court would decide impartially between members of the two groups. The peasants, moreover, must retain all the land which at present they farmed for their own account. Lastly, compensation to the owners should be paid by the exchequer, although it might later be recovered from the peasants. These proposals —particularly the suggestion that the peasants should retain all land which they held at present—were judged harmful and dangerous. The Tsar accepted the verdict of the Committee. Kavelin lost his position as tutor to the Tsarevich; the censor who had passed the offending articles received a reprimand. The Committee itself drew up a circular which laid down that in future all discussion of the peasant question must be limited to the official programme. With the circular of May 4, 1858, all serious discussion of liberation in the Russian press came to an end.

The Tsar, having made important concessions to the 'planters', was now anxious that some progress should be made. He took one of the heroic decisions of his career and resolved to tour the provinces of northern Russia to appeal in person to the local nobility for support for his policy of liberation. He was away from St. Petersburg for a month. His first stop was at Tver, where he was, perhaps, least likely to meet with a hostile reception. "I now entrust to you", he told the nobles, "a matter important to you as it is to me, that of the peasants. I rely on you to justify my confidence. The duty of dealing with this important matter has been laid on men elected from your midst. Use your best judgment, reflect carefully, seek the most advantageous manner of placing the peasantry in a new situation, make your arrangements to suit local conditions, in a manner offensive neither to the peasants nor to yourselves, on the basis of the fundamental principles which I have laid down in my Rescripts. You know how close to my heart is your welfare; I hope that the well-being of your peasants is no less dear to you." Five days later, in addressing the nobility of the province of Kostroma, Alexander repeated the key phrases of his campaign. On August 31, he spoke to the nobles of Nizhni, on

September 4 to those of Vladimir. On the 12th he addressed severe reproaches to the recalcitrant nobility of the Moscow province. On the 15th there followed a speech in a persuasive tone at Smolensk; three days later yet another at Vilna. Wherever Alexander went, he announced that deputies would be called to St. Petersburg for the final deliberations.

The Tsar's tour marks a turning-point in the development of the peasant question. It gave him an opportunity to declare in public his determination to carry the matter to a successful conclusion. His own impressions, moreover, were on the whole encouraging; he gained the conviction that there would be no systematic obstruction. Wherever he had gone he had found at least a minority of the nobility sympathetic to liberation on the terms laid down by the government.[1] The 'people' everywhere had shown its delight at the prospect of emancipation. Returning to St. Petersburg in an optimistic mood, the Tsar said to Lanskoy: "You and I have jointly started this peasant matter; we will see it through together."

Almost at the same time as Alexander, Rostovtsev had returned to St. Petersburg after a prolonged sojourn in Germany. For some time he had been conscious of his lack of intimate knowledge of the problem and had therefore determined to spend some time thinking it over. The conclusions he reached largely coincided with those already reached by the Tsar. In consequence, from this moment until his death in 1860, Rostovtsev became the Tsar's *alter ego* in the struggle for liberation. Now, in consultation with Rostovtsev and Lanskoy, Alexander decided to have their joint policy put forward in the Main Committee under his own presidency.

Meanwhile, a change had occurred in the Commit-

[1] It is, however, worth noting that the Tsar during his tour did not visit the 'planters'' strongholds in the Black Earth Belt. He confined himself to provinces where economic conditions made liberation with land less offensive to the nobility.

tee's composition. Earlier in the year, infuriated by the obstructionist tactics of the majority, the Grand-Duke Constantine had lost his temper. He told Orlov that he "greatly doubted the sincerity of these gentlemen who ... instead of removing difficulties, did what they could to increase them". When Orlov rejoined that this was an aspersion on the honour of the Russian nobility, the Grand-Duke declared that the Russian nobility were not even good enough for him to spit on. (According to another version, he merely observed that there was no such thing as a true nobility in Russia.) The members protested to the Tsar, and early in October Constantine left for a naval cruise in the Mediterranean.

In his place, the Tsar himself assumed an active role in the Main Committee. For four important meetings in October and November, he never left the chair. He declared that as the first projects of the provincial committees were beginning to reach St. Petersburg, he would lay down certain principles. From the first moment the new law was published, the peasants must gain the feeling that there had been a definite improvement in their lot. At the same time, the landowners must see that their interests had been safeguarded. The firmness and vigilance of the local authorities must not be relaxed for one moment; no disturbances of any kind must be tolerated. The Minister of the Interior should ask all provincial committees to submit, together with their projects, detailed memoranda on the way in which the peasants' lot would be bettered by their proposals. Moreover, as projects reached the Ministry of the Interior, they should be studied individually to make sure that they did not depart from the principles laid down by the government, and examined to see how far and in what manner they improved the condition of the private serfs.

Having laid down the procedure to be followed, the government had to wait for the local committees to complete their work. In these, bitter battles were raging among the members, representing at least three distinct points of view. Diehard 'planters' everywhere were fighting a rearguard action to save all land for the gentry. On the other hand, influential and well-educated nobles, including, as a rule, the members appointed by the Governors, were ready to co-operate wholeheartedly with the government in the implementation of its programme. Between the two groups stood those—and they formed the majority in most committees—whose sole desire was to save for their order the maximum of material advantage.

The divisions in the committees led to inconveniences not anticipated by the government. In the first place, they were productive of delay: hardly a single committee was able to submit its project by the date appointed. More serious was the fact that most provincial committees produced two, sometimes three, different projects. This meant a great deal of extra work for the sub-committee set up to examine them. And since two of its four members (Panin and Muraviev) were bitter opponents of liberation, the sub-committee threatened to become an impassable bottleneck.

Foreseeing this difficulty, Lanskoy had already recommended replacing the sub-committee by two Commissions under the auspices of his own Ministry. One of these would deal with principles common to all the projects, the other with local peculiarities. On February 16, 1859, the Tsar accepted the suggestion, and Rostovtsev, himself favourable to the new scheme, became president of the two Commissions. Prominent among the members were Lanskoy's assistants, Miliutin and Soloviev. Miliutin from the start was one of the key members. In March, when a vacancy occurred for the post of Deputy Minister of the Interior, Lanskoy at once recommended his indefatigable assistant. The Tsar, who did not know Miliutin personally, was only too familiar with his reputation among the 'planters' as a red revolutionary. The Grand-Duchess Helen, who passionately supported Miliutin, arranged that he should be privately presented to the Empress Mary. "This is Mirabeau beginning his secret meetings with Marie-Antoinette", the 'planters' at Court murmured after their first meeting. The Empress was able to dispel the Tsar's distrust; he appointed the 'red' official Acting Deputy Minister. Rostovtsev, who respected Miliutin's knowledge and sincerity, followed his advice in the selection of 'experts' from the provincial committees. In consequence, the members invited to join the Commissions belonged almost invariably to the liberal minorities of the provincial committees. Among the most prominent were the Slavophils, Samarin and Cherkassky. Some opponents of liberation also found a place; in spite of their inclusion, however, the Commissions were the first official bodies in Russia which had an 'abolitionist' majority. This fact, more than anything else, assured that the emancipation was finally carried out on terms not too widely divergent from those laid down by the government.

The bulk of the work fell on the shoulders of Miliutin. The Acting Deputy Minister of the Interior possessed outstanding ability, unrivalled knowledge of the problems, and a capacity for hard work. Rostovtsev jokingly described him as 'our Egeria'. The two men—the prime architects of liberation—soon agreed to combine the two Commissions into one (known as the Editing Commission), which was then subdivided into separate sections to study the administrative, economic, judicial, and financial aspects of liberation. This was the body on which would finally fall the task of drafting the emancipation laws.

On March 18, such members of the Commission as had already reached St. Petersburg, were presented to the Emperor. Alexander expressed the hope that they would successfully complete their task. He added: "All I desire is the good of Russia. You are called upon, gentlemen, to accomplish a great task. I shall know

how to value your efforts. The matter, I know, is delicate. My choice has fallen on you: I have heard about
each of you from your president; he has recommended
every one of you. I am convinced that you love Russia
as I love her and will honourably do your duty. You
will justify the confidence I place in you." Rostovtsev
would report to him regularly on their progress. "I hope
that, together, we shall bring this work to a successful
conclusion. May God help you in this difficult task; I
will not forget you. Farewell." Then, after kissing Rostovtsev, Alexander left the hall.

The first meetings of the Commission showed that
Rostovtsev's ideas had evolved in a liberal direction.
He now recommended liberation with land, a redemption operation assisted by the government, and the reduction to a minimum of the period intervening between serfdom and complete liberation. Soon a
difference of opinion arose between the majority and
the 'planters' led by P. P. Shuvalov (Marshal of
Nobility of St. Petersburg) and Prince Paskievich (son
of the former Field-Marshal). Rostovtsev, on the Tsar's
behalf, had explained that the period of transition was
to end as soon as the redemption of homestead and
allotment was completed. The principle had been
accepted by the Commission, but the 'planters' objected
that the land should remain the legal property of the
present owners, whilst the peasants should enjoy the
right of hereditary use. They insisted on recording a
minority opinion. When the Tsar ruled that this
opinion was not to be included in the printed minutes
of the Commission but simply to be appended to its
final report, they asked leave to resign. The minority
view became the subject of a bitter discussion in a
plenary meeting of the Commission. Miliutin, Soloviev,
and Cherkassky, in opposing the 'planters', argued
that the arrangement proposed by the minority
would simply continue serfdom in a modified form.
Unless the peasants were made owners of their

allotments, their economic dependence would continue, and their 'freedom' would have little meaning. On receiving the minutes of the discussion, Alexander ordered that the views of the majority should prevail. However, Shuvalov and Paskievich "sacrificing their personal views" should remain in the Commission and "participate in its labours with their former energy". The decision, typical of Alexander's methods, foreshadows the appointment of Panin as Rostovtsev's successor as President of the Editing Commission.

Shortly after this incident, the Tsar received a letter from Paskievich, once more re-stating his views. Alexander's comments reveal what his own opinions were. Where Paskievich observed that it appeared to be the government's intention to convert the serfs into landed proprietors, the Tsar wrote that this was a fundamental condition from which nothing would induce him to recede. Against some comment on the right of the peasants to refuse to acquire land Alexander observed: "After which the owners would chase them off the land and leave them to roam the country." Where Paskievich noted that the proposals of the majority could be introduced only by force, Alexander commented: "Yes, if the nobility persist in their obstinacy." A recommendation that full personal freedom should be granted only three years after the publication of the statute provoked the rejoinder: "From the very first day of publication." However, Alexander did agree that redemption must be voluntary. Where Paskievich protested his sincerity, the Emperor regretted "the false point of view". Paskievich's protests remained without result. His had been a rearguard action on behalf of liberation without land. It had been defeated by the majority in the Editing Commission supported by the Tsar. From this time onwards, the 'planters' would fight no longer about the principle of liberation with land but about the size of the allotments.

In the meantime, attention had shifted once again to

the provincial committees. By the end of July the great majority of these had completed their drafts. In almost every case, two separate projects were submitted, representing respectively the views of the 'planter' majority and of the 'liberal' minority. The Minister of the Interior tried to arrange that of the two deputies to be sent to St. Petersburg from each committee, one should represent the views of the minority. At the same time, Lanskoy warned the Tsar that the deputies of the majorities would attempt to undo the work of the Commission. They might even try to organize a 'planters'' party. The committees, therefore, should be informed that the fundamental principles of the reform were settled once and for all, and that the deputies would discuss only their local application. Alexander expressed agreement; the last struggle with the nobility was approaching.

In September deputies from twenty-one provinces were called to the capital. The arrival of the remainder had been delayed for some months until the departure of the first group. "No notables! I want no 1789," the Tsar exclaimed in conversation with Bismarck. The deputies, moreover, at the first plenary meeting, received from the lips of Rostovtsev an imperial order defining and limiting their functions. They were to have no right of initiative, but would simply answer in writing questions submitted to them by the Commission. If invited to do so, they would attend its meetings for further explanations.

Irked by these restrictions, the deputies gathered at the house of Shuvalov. An address to the Emperor was drawn up, complaining of the Ministry of the Interior and the Editing Commission, and alleging that these bodies were misrepresenting his intentions. The deputies requested permission to lay their views before the Main Committee. In the end, the idea of an address was abandoned. Instead, the deputies asked for permission to hold a joint meeting. They were told that they might

meet, unofficially, but must not discuss the general principles of the liberation. They must limit their discussions to the best manner of applying these principles
in their respective localities. Any views they might express must deal with individual provinces only. Any
representations they chose to make would be placed
before the Main Committee.

On September 16 Alexander himself addressed the
deputies. "I have called you together", he declared, "to
co-operate in a task equally important for all of us and
involving Russia's future well-being." When one of the
deputies, with greater patriotism than truthfulness, replied that they were ready to sacrifice even a third of
their property, the Tsar replied : "No, I don't ask such
a heavy sacrifice. I want this great work to be accomplished in a manner not hurtful to anyone and satisfactory to all." This remark, like others made on several
occasions, suggests that Alexander either did not fully
understand what was involved in the discussions, or was
the prisoner of his favourite phrase about a settlement
satisfactory to both parties.

In fact, no such settlement lay within the realm of
possibility. There was a fundamental clash of interests
between the peasants and the nobility. The former considered that all the land rightfully belonged to them.
The bulk of the gentry equally claimed all the land for
themselves. It was, therefore, absolutely certain from
the start that there could be no solution satisfactory to
both the main classes of Russian society. The best Alexander could hope to achieve would be to impose by his
autocratic power a compromise which, while leaving
both classes dissatisfied, would at least safeguard the
future of the empire.

Having addressed the deputies, Alexander left St.
Petersburg. During his absence, friction between the
deputies and the Commission increased. The deputies
bitterly resented an announcement from the Ministry of
the Interior that, once they had answered the questions

submitted to them, their task would be at an end. Rostovtsev, in a report to the Tsar, explained that while the
Commission looked at the matter from the point of view
of public law and the needs of the state, the deputies
took their stand on civil law and private interests. "They
are right from their own point of view—we from ours."
It was quite untrue—although widely asserted by the
landowners—that the Commission wished to rob them,
and that many of its members were 'reds'. In fact, the
principal object of the Commission was to save Russia;
the best means to that end was to liberate the serfs. No
compromise was possible between the rival points of
view.

The deputies were unable to challenge the Tsar's
authority. However, wishing to place their views on
record, several addressed themselves to the Emperor.
Eighteen declared that the proposals of the Commission reflected neither the general need nor the
principles established by the Tsar. They asked that before the project was finally submitted to the Main
Committee, the provincial deputies should be allowed
to express their views. Another five deputies, representing the liberal minorities, declared that the present proposals would ruin the owners without helping the
peasants. They called for the transfer of land to the
peasants by means of an immediate redemption operation. One deputy appealed to the Tsar to call an
assembly of the Russian nobility which, under his own
presidency, would take the final decisions.

These proposals, especially the ones for an elective
national assembly, were unacceptable to Alexander.
"He has fully convinced me", he wrote on one of the
petitions, "that he and those who think like him wish to
establish in our country an oligarchic form of government." The Tsar decided to transmit the different
addresses to the Main Committee. That body resolved
to silence the inconvenient spokesmen of Russian
opinion. All signatories of petitions, regardless of

the views expressed, received official reprimands. The deputies dispersed.

The meeting of the first group of deputies in St. Petersburg throws a vivid light on one of the basic problems facing the Tsar. From the beginning he had spared no effort to enlist the co-operation of the gentry. He had at every stage encouraged it to take an active part in working out the details of the proposed reform. Yet, however much he would have liked to carry through the measure with the free consent of the nobility, he had never been able to permit real freedom of discussion. The majorities in the provincial committees, like the majority of the deputies, were fundamentally opposed to liberation, and would have obstructed it if they could. The liberal minorities, on the other hand, not only went farther in their sympathy for the peasants than appeared practicable to the government, but were calling for a variety of far-reaching reforms in Russian public life. It might well appear to the Tsar that public participation in preparing the liberation statute, except within the narrowest limits, was incompatible with the orderly introduction of the reform.

The incident also reveals the importance of the autocracy in defending the interests of the serfs. Those interests were safer in the hands of Alexander and Rostovtsev, Lanskoy, and Miliutin, than in those of any elected assembly possible in Russia at that time. It is easy to imagine what would have happened to liberation in a 'constitutional' assembly dominated by the 'planters' and their friends. The truth was that co-operation between the autocrat and the reformers in the Ministry of the Interior against the 'planters' in the provincial committees and on the Main Committee offered the only chance of an effective reform.

The dismissal of the first group of deputies—the second was to be of purely formal importance—marked the discomfiture of the provincial gentry. From now on the battle would be waged at the centre between Rostovtsev's Editing Commission and Orlov's Main Committee. In these circumstances much would depend on the Emperor himself, who held the casting vote between the rival bodies. Rostovtsev was now beginning to take to heart the slanders circulating at Court against himself and the Editing Commission. In a letter to the Tsar, he defended the conduct of his colleagues. Alexander, in his reply, tried to raise his adjutant's flagging spirits. "If these gentlemen consider that they can frighten me by means of these insinuations, they will find they are grossly mistaken. I am far too convinced of the justice of our sacred cause to allow them to arrest me in its accomplishment. The great question is how to carry out the measure. In this, now as always, I place my trust in God and rely on the help of those who, like yourself, sincerely desire the success of the measure. On its success depend the salvation and future well-being of Russia. Do not lose heart, just as I do not despond, although I, too, have much grief to bear. Let us pray God together that he may give us strength. I embrace you with all my heart."

Alexander's sympathetic encouragement could no longer save Rostovtsev. In November, the first symptoms appeared of the illness which was to carry him to the grave. Soon he was confined to his house where, however, he continued to preside over meetings of the Commission. During December he received three visits from his imperial master. Early in the new year he took to his bed. As his illness grew worse, the Tsar's visits became increasingly frequent. Alexander had given instructions that all worry was to be kept from the patient, but Rostovtsev would not hear of it. He had asked his doctor to tell him when his case became hopeless, as there was some work he wished to complete. Thus he devoted his last remaining energies to drawing up a memorandum which would be for the Tsar a clear and non-technical guide to the elaborate statute which was taking shape in the Commission. Early on February 18 he died, with the Emperor praying at his bedside. Alexander himself, together with members of the imperial family, carried the coffin part of the way to its last resting-place.

On the day after the funeral, Semenov, Rostovtsev's closest collaborator, handed the Tsar the latter's memorandum. Alexander confided to Semenov that he did not know whom to appoint in Rostovtsev's place. He had thought of consulting the dying man, but delicacy had stopped him. In any case, whoever succeeded Rostovtsev, the work would be carried on in his spirit. "I ask you to reassure your colleagues. I shall not withdraw from anything laid down in the writings of our late friend, who has so honourably carried out my intentions. Not only will I permit no change in the membership of the Commission, but I guarantee the completion of the work in accordance with the views of the majority. There will be no interference from the new president of the Commission. I ask you, the fellow-workers of the deceased, to complete the work in the spirit in which you have conducted it until now." Four days later, Rostovtsev's successor was named. His name sent a chill down the spine of every supporter of liberation. It was . . . Count V. N. Panin, the Minister of Justice.

Few acts of Alexander II have aroused more criticism than his decision to entrust to Panin the presidency of the Editing Commission. Yet the choice was neither as illogical nor as unreasonable as has been made to appear. Clearly, Rostovtsev's successor must be found among the circle of men who for the last three years had by constant work on emancipation become familiar with the manifold details involved. As the Tsar's representative, he must also be a personage of importance. The choice, therefore, was limited. The aged Lanskoy—hated by the 'planters'—could never have steered the statute through a hostile Main Com-

mittee. The Grand-Duke Constantine, owing to his prolonged absence, was out of touch with the work of legislation. In his case also, as in that of Lanskoy, co-operation with the Main Committee was unthinkable. No
other prominent 'reformer' existed. If the new president
had, on the other hand, to be found among the
'planters', Panin was the obvious choice. Educated and
intelligent, he was regarded as a man of honour. His
position as Minister of Justice recommended him for a
difficult appointment. Alexander felt that he was a
man to be trusted. Politically, the appointment had important advantages. It established closer links between
the Editing Commission and the Main Committee. It
seemed likely to reduce obstruction in the latter body.
It helped to calm the apprehensions of the gentry. If
Panin loyally carried out the Tsar's orders, the appointment, in spite of its apparent inconsistency, was a wise
one.

The Tsar did all in his power to assure that Panin
would carry on the work in the spirit of Rostovtsev. He
told him that nothing must be changed in the working
of the Commission. His predecessor's political testament
must be his guide. "I entrust this matter to you on the
terms on which we agreed. Conduct it, as it has been
conducted. I have always thought of you as an honest
man; it never entered my mind that you could deceive
me." Panin afterwards assured the Grand-Duke Constantine that, whatever his personal views, he would
subordinate them to the wishes of the Tsar. Actually,
he later made more than one attempt to alter the spirit
of the legislation prepared by the late Rostovtsev. If the
statute which finally emerged still retained much of its
original spirit, the result was due less to Panin's honesty
than to the Tsar's vigilance and determination.

In July the Commission began the codification of its
project. The Tsar laid down that the work must be completed by October 22, 1860. On that date, the Commission was disbanded after an expression of gratitude

from the Emperor. In his closing speech Alexander used a dangerous expression. "It may be", he declared, "that many changes will still need to be made; in any case, however, you have the honour of having done the first work, and Russia will be grateful to you." The Tsar well knew that at least one major hurdle remained—to get the statute adopted by the Main Committee. To do so, he had made an important move. A little while before, Orlov, its aged president, had fallen seriously ill. Alexander, thereupon, had appointed the Grand-Duke Constantine in his place.

Constantine's task in the Committee was not an easy one. Three different views were expressed. Prince Gagarin, an isolated Don Quixote, still spoke for landless liberation. The 'planters' led by Muraviev wished to modify the draft statute in the interest of the owners. Finally, a group led by Lanskoy, Chevkin (Minister of Communications), and Bludov (President of the Imperial Council) wished to accept the draft statute with a minimum of modifications. Panin's attitude was ambiguous. In fact, those who wished to introduce substantial alterations were in the majority. It was the personal influence of the imperial brothers which prevented major changes. At the crucial moment, Constantine succeeded in convincing Panin, and Alexander Adlerberg Junior. Their defection deprived the 'planters' of their majority, and the statute was accepted without major alterations.

Only one further stage of the long-drawn-out legislative procedure now remained—discussion of the statute in the Imperial Council. Before this body the Tsar, in introducing the draft, made an urgent plea for haste. The matter had now been dragging on for four years. On the surface, his good people still showed admirable calm and restraint. But fears and hopes were widespread among serfs and owners alike. He was happy that the first initiative had come from the nobility (a polite fiction), and he had done all in his power to reduce the sacrifices demanded of them. They must not, however, forget that the situation of the serfs must be improved, and not on paper alone. The abolition of serfdom was vital to the future strength of Russia. The matter must be concluded forthwith, as any further delay might prove fatal to the empire. He would listen to different views and was ready to accept amendments. However, he had a right to demand one thing—that they would act not as landowners but as statesmen, disregarding personal interests, and as statesmen, moreover, entrusted with his confidence. Before the agricultural season began, the task must be completed.

With great rapidity, the Council set to work to discuss the one-thousand-odd sections of the statute. Where there was a division, the extreme 'planters' led by Gagarin could muster 8 votes, the moderate critics under Muraviev 16, and the defenders of the statute as it stood 29. On many points of detail, however, the last group was placed in a minority. In that event, the Tsar, as a rule, decided in their favour. However, to speed up the labours of the Council, he accepted one last reduction in the maximum size of allotments. More serious, he failed to veto a proposal introduced at the instance of Gagarin, which created the gratuitous or 'beggarly' allotment. This allotment equalling a quarter of the legal maximum for any given province could, with the peasants' consent, be allocated to them without any redemption payment, while the owner at the same time waived all claim to compensation. Owners of fertile soil would later feel tempted to press these allotments—which meant slow but inexorable starvation for those who accepted them—upon their former serfs.

On February 19/March 3, the sixth anniversary of his accession, Alexander signed the statute. The news was announced to the Russian people in an insincere manifesto drawn up in archaic Russian by the Metropolitan Philaret, an enemy of liberation. On Sunday,

March 17, it was read from the pulpit in all the churches of the capital. In one place it was read publicly by the Tsar himself. Special envoys carried the news to the provinces. On March 24, the Tsar addressed a crowd outside the Winter Palace : "The work was already begun in the time of my father, but he was unable to accomplish it in his lifetime. With God's help, it fell to my lot to complete the task for your good. Now, my children, go and thank God; pray for the eternal repose of my father; prove yourselves useful to the fatherland." All who had taken an official part in the work of liberation received a medal with the inscription 'I thank you'.

Accounts of the way in which the news was received in the capital differ. Kropotkin has left a description of his own impressions. He was in bed at the Corps of Cadets on Sunday, March 17, when his batman, Ivanov, dashed in with the tea-tray, shouting: "Prince, freedom! The manifesto is posted on the Gostinny Dvor" (the block of shops opposite the Corps). "Did you see it yourself?" "Yes. People stand round; one reads, the others listen. It *is* freedom!" In a couple of minutes, Kropotkin was out of bed and dressed. A comrade rushed in : "Kropotkin, freedom!" he shouted. "Here is the manifesto. My uncle learnt last night that it would be read at the early Mass at the Isaac Cathedral; so we went. There were not many people there; peasants only. The manifesto was read and distributed after the Mass. They well understood what it meant. When I came out of the church two peasants, who stood in the gateway, said to me in such a droll way: 'Well, sir? Now—all gone?' " Kropotkin himself read and re-read the manifesto, written in an elevated style in a useless mixture of Russian and Church Slavonic which obscured its sense. The liberty was not immediate, the serfs would remain serfs two years longer. Yet the main point stood out: the serfs were liberated, they would get their homesteads and allotments. They would have to pay a price, but slavery was at an end.

They went on parade. When the military part was over, the Tsar, remaining on horseback, called out: "The officers to me!" They gathered round him. In a loud voice, he addressed them on the great event of the day. Kropotkin and his friends—not yet officers—only heard scraps of the speech: "The officers . . . the representatives of the nobility in the army . . . an end has been put to centuries of injustice. . . . I expect sacrifices from the nobility . . . the loyal nobility will gather around the throne. . . ." There were enthusiastic hurrahs from the officers at the end.

As soon as the parade was over, Kropotkin dashed home to change in time for the Italian opera. Several young cadets dashed lightfooted up to the 'gods'. The house was crowded. In the first interval, the smoking-room was filled with excited young men, who all addressed each other whether acquainted or not. The sound of music reached their ears—they rushed back to the hall. The band was playing the National Anthem, 'God Save the Tsar'—drowned almost immediately in enthusiastic hurrahs from the galleries, the boxes, the pit. There was the same enthusiasm in the streets. Crowds of peasants and educated men stood in front of the palace cheering. Wherever the Tsar appeared, he was followed by cheering crowds.

Kropotkin's impressions were recorded long after the event, and it is possible that his memory deceived him. A Prussian diplomat, at all events, who witnessed the same scenes, wrote to his family shortly afterwards: "When on Sunday, March 17/5, the liberation was proclaimed, I went at noon to the cathedral of St. Isaac. The apathy of the public was positively ridiculous. What the papers write about enthusiasm is untrue. In the theatres the anthem was played, that is all. The following Sunday, outside the Winter Palace, a few thousand muzhiks presented to the emperor bread and salt (the traditional ceremony of Russian peasants welcoming their master) and, last Sunday, some deputations arrived from Moscow and other towns." It is more than likely that Kropotkin, regarding the matter subjectively and in retrospect, exaggerated the extent of popular enthusiasm.

At all events, as soon as the details of the complicated emancipation statute began to be understood, any enthusiasm which might have been felt rapidly evaporated. The terms of the liberation were a compromise which could satisfy neither of the main social groups. In spite of all modifications introduced for its benefit, the nobility, at a conservative estimate, lost roughly one-third of its land. Some estimates, probably exaggerated, put the figure as high as three-fifths. Article 8 of the statute did indeed promise that this act of confiscation would never be repeated; but for the landowners even this single measure was an unprecedented act of robbery. By this time, the financial situation of many of them was far from rosy. They were deep in debt; some seven-tenths of the privately owned serfs on the eve of the emancipation were mortgaged to state credit institutions. To pay their debts the owners entered into agreements with the peasant communities on their estates for the transfer of land to the peasants; after which they received from the exchequer government bonds to compensate them for their losses. During the first decade following liberation, some 70 per cent of the owners concluded such agreements. Of the sum of 588 million roubles due to them as compensation, they received a mere 326—the rest was retained to pay their debts to public credit institutions. Moreover, the bonds in which the government paid compensation depreciated in value. This reduced the net proceeds to some 230 million roubles. Thanks to its improvident and spendthrift habits, the Russian nobility rapidly spent these and began once again to live on borrowed money. By 1870 the total indebtedness (some 250 million roubles) already exceeded the net proceeds from compensation payments. In general, the nobility and gentry, already deep in debt, were impoverished by the liberation without even the consolation of increased political influence.

The peasants, although as free men they gained greatly in self-esteem, found their economic condition only marginally improved. The charges imposed upon them under the Act of Emancipation were grossly in excess alike of the yield of their land and of its value. The average size of the new allotments, except in the western provinces, fell well below that of their pre-reform holdings. This loss, as might have been expected, was particularly marked in the fertile southern and south-western provinces. In one of these it was estimated at 42 per cent, and the average loss may well have been in the neighbourhood of one-third. Moreover, the larger pre-emancipation allotments had occupied only half the serf's time; for three days in the week he had worked on his master's estate. Now the reduced allotments should, in theory at least, provide him with whole-time employment. By 1878, according to the figures of the Central Statistical Committee, only 13 per cent of the former private serfs were well-endowed with land. Something over 40 per cent were adequately provided for, whilst the remainder did not have sufficient land to sustain themselves and their families. An added difficulty lay in the fact that by the liberation the peasants lost their customary right to timber and firewood from manorial forests, and were denied the use of meadows and pastures which the landowners often retained in their own possession. Many peasant families rapidly sank into debt. A particularly sad fate awaited the majority of household serfs. They got no land, and would hardly have known what to do with it had it been given to them. They obtained immediate personal freedom but nothing else. Most left their former masters to seek employment elsewhere. Some were engaged by merchants, proud to employ the former coachmen and cooks of princes. Those who had learnt a trade found employment in the towns. The rest faced an uncertain and often miserable future.

The peasants soon realized that the land and freedom they had received was not what they had hoped for and vaguely considered their due. Many consoled themselves with the idea that this was not yet the true liberation; another would follow at the end of the two-year period of 'temporary obligation'. Alexander himself had to contradict these rumours. Later in the year he told a group of peasants: "Reports have reached me that you expect a new emancipation. There will be no emancipation except the one I have given you. Obey the laws and the statutes! Work and toil! Obey the authorities and the landowners!" It was cold comfort for the peasantry. Acts of insubordination increased immediately after the liberation, often due to misunderstandings. The most serious incident took place at Bezdna in the province of Pensa, where peasants, misled by a religious fanatic, started a demonstration. Unarmed but obstinate, they returned to obedience only in the face of an infantry volley. Fifty peasants were killed and over 300 wounded. However, stern repression, combined with exemplary fairness shown by most of the 'mediators' charged with applying the reform on the spot, usually young noblemen of liberal sympathies, soon calmed the excitement among the peasants. In the years following the emancipation, most experienced some improvement in their circumstances.

The terms of the liberation came as a disappointment to the liberals and radicals who had greeted with such delight the Tsar's decision to liberate the serfs. As early as 1858, Chernyshevsky expressed regret at the premature confidence he had expressed in the Tsar. After the massacre of Bezdna, students in many universities, sometimes encouraged by professors, organized protest demonstrations. They expressed the feelings of the radical intelligentsia. From this disappointment at the terms of liberation can be dated the beginning of the revolutionary movement which would one day kill the 'Tsar Liberator' and finally destroy his dynasty.

Later historians have criticized the terms of the emancipation as placing an undue burden on the shoulders of the newly-liberated peasantry and blamed the Tsar for failing to curb the 'planters'. Others have argued that since serfdom had already become 'un-economical' and was, in any case, beginning to abolish itself from below, the statute of 1861 did little more than register an accomplished fact. Both views overlook the persistent opposition to liberation with land encountered by the Tsar not only in the Main Committee but also in the provincial committees of the nobility. The measure was carried through in the teeth of bitter hostility: to get for the peasants even the terms finally obtained was not an easy matter : without constant pressure from the Tsar, liberation with land was unthinkable. There is much truth in Tolstoy's remark on the occasion of a toast to Alexander II, the 'Tsar Liberator' : "I drink this toast with particular pleasure. No others are needed, for in reality we owe the Emancipation to the Emperor alone."

Alexander himself was disappointed at the reception of the Liberation Statute. Less than a month after its publication, Lanskoy was allowed to retire on account of his advanced age. With him went Nicholas Miliutin, the chief architect of liberation. "I am sorry to part with you", Alexander told him, "but I must; the nobility describe you as one of the reds." Lanskoy's place was taken by Valuiev, whose sympathies were on the side of the nobility and its demands for greater political influence.

At the same time, Alexander understood perfectly that the liberation of the serfs must of necessity lead to a series of further reforms. If he had handed over the Ministry of the Interior to the 'oligarchs', this did not mean that the reformers had lost the day. On the contrary, the star of the Grand-Duke Constantine was again

in the ascendant. During the autumn and winter of
1861 and in the following spring, several of his followers
(the 'Konstantinovtsy') received important appointments. Thus Dimitry Miliutin, the brother of Nicholas,
a brilliant and highly educated staff officer of extreme
democratic convictions, replaced an aged nonentity as
Minister of War. Golovnin, a radical-liberal and the
Grand-Duke's right-hand man, became Minister of
Education. Reutern, a financial expert and an ardent
reformer, became Minister of Finance. Panin's place as
Minister of Justice was taken by a reformer, Zamiatnin.
Bludov, a supporter of liberation, became President of
both the Imperial Council and the Council of Ministers.
His place at the head of the Second Division of the
Imperial Chancery, which dealt with drafting legislation, was taken by Baron Korff, another friend of reform. With these appointments, the stage was set for the
second phase of Alexander's 'great reforms'. In its New
Year issue for 1862 the *Northern Post*, organ of the
Ministry of the Interior, announced that the government was studying plans for a number of important
changes. These included a general reform of the judicial system, a complete reorganization of the police, an
improved method of presenting budgets and keeping
official accounts, a reform in the administration of
imperial domains, and the development of elementary education. A complete transformation of the
organs of local government might have been added to
the list. It was a programme which would have been
unthinkable in the days of Nicholas I.

*Chapter Four*

# The Reforming Emperor

THE liberation of the serfs was undoubtedly the most spectacular achievement of Alexander's reign, yet it was only one of a number of major reforms. In some respects, indeed, it was only a beginning; its repercussions were felt in every department of Russian life. It was the reforms following the Act of 1861 which developed the break with feudalism by reducing the class privileges of the nobility. By the same token, the later reforms raised the status of the non-noble part of the population and paved the way for more rapid commercial and industrial development. The changes brought about in Russia after 1861 'modernized' the *ancien régime* by bringing it more closely into line with western European practices and ideas. They were Russia's response to the challenge of Sevastopol.

In the later reforms, the Tsar's personal share was somewhat less prominent than it had been in the struggle for liberation. This was due principally to the fact that the later changes encountered less opposition. None of the later reforms seriously touched the property rights of individuals and classes. Again, several were the direct and necessary complement to the liberation, and thus no longer the subject of discussion. Alexander's wholesale appointment of reforming Ministers between November 1861 and the following January meant that the reforming party in the government was now stronger than it had been. Finally, between 1861 and 1864 reforming policies were in the ascendant to such an extent that even inveterate 'planters' were carried

83

away by the tide. In these circumstances, direct personal intervention by the Tsar in the legislative process
had become less necessary.

This, however, is not to say that the Tsar's over-all
influence did not remain decisive. His was the initiative
for all new legislation. He normally laid down the scope
of the reform it was intended to introduce. After the
appropriate Ministry had elaborated in some detail the
general principles of the new measure, they would again
be submitted to the Tsar. Once the draft had been completed, usually by a ministerial committee, it was again
laid before the Emperor, who would sanction its submission to the Imperial Council. Finally, an imperial
ukase explaining the scope and intention of the new law
would accompany its notification to the Governing
Senate. Moreover, whenever differences arose during
the preparation of a new measure, the final decision was
made by the Tsar. Alexander, therefore, exercised a
constant supervision over all the reforms of his reign.

In addition to his administrative supervision, the
Tsar exercised political control. He selected his Ministers, who were responsible to him alone. He was his own
Prime Minister : in 1861, he dismissed Lanskoy and N.
Miliutin, and gave the important Ministry of the Interior to Valuiev, representative of the 'liberalizing'
nobility. Some months later, he entrusted to radical reformers the Ministries of Education, Justice, War, and
Finance. The political reaction after the attempt on his
life in 1866, which might easily have ended all reform,
did not, in fact, produce a wholesale dismissal of reforming Ministers. Reformers and 'liberals' did lose
control of the 'political' Ministries—Justice, Education,
and the Interior. The process, however, was gradual. In
the 'technical' departments of War and Finance, reformers remained firmly in control. The radical demo-
crat at the Ministry of War, in spite of severe attacks,
was retained by Alexander to the end. Politically, the

later reforms no less than the liberation of 1861 were the work of the autocratic power.

The moving spirit behind those reforms, however, was less the Tsar himself than his brother, the Grand-Duke Constantine. Minister of Marine from the beginning of the reign, Constantine had from the start been the protagonist of radical reform. He had instructed his subordinates to give up the 'official lie' of reporting that all was well when the reverse was the case. Naval courts-martial had been reformed, cruel punishments discontinued, educational institutions developed. The *Naval Almanack,* official organ of the Ministry, had, under the editorship of Golovnin, become the most outspoken paper in Russia. It discussed legal reforms and educational changes. Abuses in the administration of the navy were pilloried. In an official circular, Constantine had offered handsome prizes for contributions criticizing 'bravely and effectively' shortcomings of naval life. The Ministry of Marine became "the nursery, the general staff of the entire reforming movement of the sixties". As President of the Geographical Society, Constantine gathered around him a group of ardent reformers—Reutern, Golovnin, the Miliutin brothers. With their appointment to ministerial office late in 1861, the stage was set for major reforms in almost every department of Russian life.

Amongst the most important of these reforms was that of the legal system. Even Nicholas I had recognized the need for this. In 1844 he had heard of some gross abuses in a tribunal not far from the Winter Palace, and had ordered an inquiry. Baron Korff, in charge of the investigation, had discovered "a yawning abyss of all possible horrors, which have been accumulating for years". The Emperor, after studying the report, had written at the bottom : "Unheard-of disgrace! The carelessness of the authority immediately concerned is incredible and unpardonable. I feel ashamed and sad that such disorder could exist almost under my eyes and remain unknown to me." Yet the projects for reform prepared by several committees under Bludov were drawn up unsystematically and no changes were made under Nicholas. A reform of the legal system had been Alexander's first promise to his subjects, contained in the manifesto announcing the conclusion of peace. Until 1861, however, he had been occupied with other matters. The liberation of the serfs made change an urgent necessity, as ways must be found to replace the vanished seigneurial jurisdiction. The reform of the legal system had become the most urgent immediate task facing the Russian Government.

Late in 1861, Alexander set up a commission of officials and jurists to work out the general principles for a radical transformation of the Russian legal system. In his instructions he told members to work out "those fundamental principles, the undoubted merit of which is at present recognized by science and the experience of Europe, in accordance with which Russia's judicial institutions must be reorganized". The direction to follow European theory and practice forms a landmark in the history of Russian law. "The Chinese Wall", a Russian historian has written, "which for forty-five years had separated our legislators from the direct influence of European science and contemporary progress, collapsed. The principles of European public law and science, which till then had penetrated into Russia only as contraband, were at last freely admitted into our legislation." The commission's report was a comprehensive indictment of the existing system, listing no fewer than twenty-five radical defects. To remove these, it proposed that the judicial organization should be completely separated from all other branches of the administration; that the fullest publicity should be introduced into the tribunals; that trial by jury should be adopted for criminal cases; that summary courts staffed by Justices of the Peace should be set up for petty cases; and that procedure in the ordinary courts should be greatly simplified. What was proposed was nothing less than the transformation of an effete and out-of-date system into a modern judicial edifice.

The fundamental principles of the reform were made public on October 10, 1862, and comments were invited from universities, officers of the law, and private individuals. No fewer than 446 observations were submitted, later published in six bulky volumes. These were taken into consideration by a new committee composed of the best jurists of the empire, which was charged with the task of preparing the detailed legislation. In eleven months these specialists had completed their labours, preparing a draft law on the establishment of new judicial institutions and draft codes of procedure in civil and criminal cases. After discussion in the Imperial Council, the judicial statutes received the imperial assent on December 2, 1864. In a ukase to the Senate announcing the fact, Alexander declared: "On ascending the throne of my ancestors, one of my first wishes publicly proclaimed in the manifesto of March 19, 1856, was : 'May justice and mercy reign in our courts !' Ever since that time, amidst other reforms called for by the needs of our national life, I have never ceased to reflect on the manner of achieving this object through a better organization of the judiciary." The present statutes were the outcome of his wish "to establish in Russia expeditious, just, merciful, and impartial courts for all our subjects; to raise the judicial authority by giving it proper independence and, in general, to increase in the people that respect for the law which national well-being requires, and which must be the constant guide of all and everyone from the highest to the lowest".

The new judicial edifice was simple and symmetrical. There were two great sections distinct from and independent of each other. On one side stood the jurisdiction of the Justices of the Peace, on the other the regular courts. Each section contained an ordinary court and a court of appeal; in the case of the peace jurisdiction, this was a counterpart of the English Quarter Sessions. The upper part of the structure, equally covering both sections, consisted of the Senate, organized as a Court of Revision—on the model of the French *Cour de Cassation*. The division of duties between the two sections of the judicature was clear. The peace courts were to decide petty cases which involved no complicated legal principles, and to settle, if possible by conciliation, the minor conflicts and disputes of everyday life. The function of the regular tribunals was to take cognizance of more serious cases. In the former courts, the judges were at first chosen from the local inhabitants by popular election (later, this function was transferred to the zemstvos), while in the more formal regular courts the judges were trained jurists nominated by the Emperor.

In 1866, the new courts were opened in the ten provinces which formed the judicial districts of St. Petersburg and Moscow. Their extension to other parts of the empire was spread over decades. There was a great shortage of trained lawyers. Moreover, after auspicious beginnings, public interest slackened. In some instances the statutes were later applied in a modified form. Thus trial by jury was not introduced in Poland, the western provinces, or the Caucasus.

The working of the new courts is described by Mackenzie Wallace, who during a stay in Russia extending from the beginning of 1870 to the end of 1875, had ample opportunity to study these courts in action. One notable feature of the reform was the immediate popularity of the peace jurisdiction. In Moscow, the authorities had calculated that under the new system the number of cases would be more than doubled, and that on an average a thousand cases a year would be heard before each Justice. Great was their surprise when, instead, the number turned out to be 2,800. In St. Petersburg and other large towns, the new courts proved equally popular. The reason for this popularity is not far to seek. Mackenzie Wallace describes the contrast between the old and the new. Under the old system, if two workmen (or peasants) brought their dispute before a police court, "they were pretty sure to get scolded in language unfit for ears polite, or to receive still worse treatment". In the peace court, the Justice, "always scrupulously polite without distinction of persons, listened patiently to the complaint, tried to arrange matters amicably and, if he failed, gave the decision at once according to law and common sense". The popularity of the peace courts increased further when people understood that they acted expeditiously, without unnecessary formalities and—above all—without bribes or blackmail.

Sometimes, indeed, the Justices carried their democratic outlook to extremes. "Imagining that their mission was to eradicate the conceptions and habits of serfage, they sometimes used their authority for giving lessons in philanthropic liberalism, and took a malicious delight in wounding the susceptibilities, and occasionally even the material interests, of those whom they regarded as enemies of the good cause." The number of such cases was not great, and it rapidly decreased. The mere possibility that justice might be partial to the underdog shows how far matters had moved since the days of Nicholas I.

In the regular courts also there was an unmistakable improvement. Wallace observed that it was not easy to find sufficient men with legal training and practical experience of the law to staff the new courts. However, he recorded, "the present generation of judges are better prepared and more capable than their predecessors". Above all, he notes that on the score of probity he had never heard any complaint. No greater contrast to the courts of Nicholas could possibly be imagined. With all their blemishes (and they were numerous), the new courts remained a lasting memorial to

Alexander II and a symbol of the new spirit which was beginning to pervade Russian public life.

The other great organic reform flowing directly from the liberation of the serfs was in the sphere of local government. In the time of serfdom the Emperor Nicholas, when referring to the landed proprietors, used to say jocularly that he had in his empire 50,000 zealous and efficient hereditary police officers. With the emancipation law the authority of these hereditary police masters disappeared; measures had to be taken to replace it. While it was intended from the start that some of the former owners' administrative duties should be transferred to the institutions of peasant self-government, it was clear that an organ would be needed to control an area larger than a village or group of villages.

The reform of the rural police had been intimately linked with the liberation of the serfs and had accordingly been considered in connection with it. In an instruction of April 6, 1859, Alexander set out the principles on which local government was to be reformed. Great administrative activity followed. The local committees on the peasant question submitted to the Main Committee and to the Editing Commission projects for the reform of local self-government, all of which were finally collected by Miliutin's Commission. That Commission soon reached agreement on the reorganization of the police. It proved more difficult, however, to agree on the plan for the creation of new organs of local government, the zemstvos.[1] Two rival views held the field. One favoured the preponderance of the nobility in the management of local affairs, the other equal participation by all the social groups. As long as Miliutin presided over the Commission, the 'democrats' had the upper hand. When Valuiev became Minister of the Interior in the spring of 1861, the balance tilted to the

[1] The word *zemstvo* is derived from *zemlia,* the Russian word for land. It is analogous to the German *Landtag,* and means an 'assembly of the land'.

side of the 'oligarchs'. It was Valuiev's policy to reserve
for the nobility the greatest possible influence in local
affairs, to place the zemstvos under the control of the
Ministry of the Interior, and to limit their activities to
the purely economic field. The project, which he
steered through the Commission, was inspired by a
double preoccupation : to make the zemstvos as inno-
cuous as possible and to ensure the preponderance of
the larger landowners.

The struggle begun in the Commission was continued
in the Imperial Council. Miliutin himself, Reutern,
Baron Korff, and other reformers attacked the principles
of Valuiev's draft. A clash occurred over the manner of
choosing zemstvo presidents. Should the president be
elected by the zemstvo assembly, or should he be the
local marshal of nobility? When the matter was discussed in relation to district zemstvos, the Council was
evenly divided. Alexander decided in favour of the
'oligarchs'. When it came to the question of the higher
provincial zemstvos, the 'democrats' were outvoted.
Korff led an impassioned attack on the provisions re-
stricting their functions, and on their subordination to
the Ministry of the Interior. "The public desire above
all, that, however limited the functions of the zemstvos,
they should have *real* independence." Although supported by D. A. Miliutin (Minister of War) and Kovalevsky (a former Minister of Education), Korff was unable to make an impression. Valuiev rejoined that the
attacks on bureaucratic interference were exaggerated;
independent zemstvos would become 'a state within the
state'. When the functions of the zemstvos were discussed, Kovalevsky proposed the inclusion of primary
education. Panin opposed the suggestion; he declared
that to entrust popular education and the responsibility
for health and prisons to these bodies would be to
encourage hopes and pretensions which it might not be
possible to satisfy. The Council decided against him.
Finally, a bitter and prolonged argument arose about

the functions of the zemstvos in relation to taxation. Prince Shcherbatov, the mayor of Moscow, supported by Reutern and Kovalevsky, pleaded for a wide zemstvo autonomy in matters of taxation—even for some voice in the disposal of imperial taxes raised in the locality. The proposals provoked a philippic from Valuiev—"To give the zemstvos a voice in matters common to the whole empire would be to break up the unitary executive power of the empire and distribute it among some forty or fifty bodies. This would expose the social order and the entire imperial structure to perils which must be apparent to everyone." After his speech the discussion became so violent that the president had to suspend the sitting. In the end a majority rejected Shcherbatov's proposals.

On January 13, 1864, Alexander II signed the zemstvo statute. The new legislation owed its distinctive character to his personal action in supporting Valuiev against the Miliutins and Reutern. In 1861, he had removed the 'democrats' from the Ministry of the Interior and handed it over to the 'oligarchs'. The new zemstvo statute was the logical and inevitable outcome of that decision, the 'consolation prize' offered to the nobility for the losses of 1861.

The zemstvos were to operate at two levels—district and provincial. They were intended to allow all classes of the population to participate in the conduct of local affairs. Members of the district zemstvo were elected for three years. The electors were divided into three classes, according to a property qualification and on the principle "that participation in the conduct of local affairs should be proportionate to everyone's economic interests". The first class included all landowners, regardless of their social class. In this class, while an estate of a certain size carried one vote, owners of smaller estates had to combine to choose an 'elector' to vote with the larger proprietors. Owners of real property, other than lands attaining a certain value, also possessed a vote.

The second, more numerous, category was composed of townsmen, whose votes also were graded according to wealth. Finally, the peasants elected their representatives by means of a special indirect system. The total membership of each zemstvo was fixed by law in such a way as to prevent the preponderance of any one social group. In fact, for the thirty-three provinces covered by the statute, the total number was fixed at 13,024. Of these, 6,204 were to be elected by the landed proprietors, 1,649 by the townsmen, and 5,171 by the peasants. The landowners, therefore, enjoyed a relative but not an absolute majority. Presently, too, the social composition of the zemstvos would be affected by the fact that non-nobles in increasing numbers were beginning to acquire estates. The provincial zemstvos, dealing with matters affecting a whole province, were elected by members of the district zemstvos from among their own number. At the higher level, there was a marked preponderance of the 'landed element'.

The zemstvos met annually, but their sessions were relatively short. They discussed the outlines of their work, debated and voted the budget, and decided their future policy. To carry out their decisions and direct their permanent secretariat, they elected for three years an executive bureau composed of a president and at least two members. The election of the president was subject to official confirmation by the Governor of the province for the district president, by the Minister of the Interior for the provincial president. The members of the bureau, elected after the president, were not subject to confirmation. The bureaux had the power to engage administrative staff, as well as the specialists necessary to deal with the various branches of regional economy and welfare. As the organization of public instruction and medical assistance required a large number of doctors and teachers, the number of these specialists rose rapidly as the zemstvos extended their activities.

However, the position of the zemstvo executives was not as strong as might appear. They had to carry out orders received from a variety of Ministries on matters like recruiting, billeting of troops, transport. In several branches of regional activity they functioned side by side with organs of the central administration. Contrary to the wishes of Baron Korff, their resolutions had no executive power. To carry out their decisions, and even to collect local taxes, they had, in the last resort, to rely on the ordinary police, which took its orders from the Governor. Only after 1873 were they given the right to make legally binding by-laws with regard to matters like sanitation or fire precautions. The spirit of Valuiev had triumphed; against the wishes of the reformers, the zemstvos had been prevented from growing into fully autonomous institutions of local self-government.

The original intention had been to set up zemstvos without delay in thirty-three provinces. In fact, during 1865 they were opened in nineteen provinces, and during the following year in another nine. By 1875, a further six had come into existence. Mackenzie Wallace, after careful observation of their work, concluded that the zemstvos fulfilled "tolerably well, without scandalous peculation and jobbery", their "commonplace and everyday duties". They had created a new and more equitable system of rating by which landed proprietors and house-owners were made to bear their share of the public burdens. They had done a good deal to provide medical aid and primary education for rural districts. They had 'improved wonderfully' the condition of the hospitals, lunatic asylums, and benevolent institutions committed to their charge. In their efforts to aid the peasantry they had helped to improve the native breeds of horses and cattle, to create a system of obligatory fire insurance, and to make provision for preventing and extinguishing fires—which was extremely important in a country where peasants lived in wooden huts, and where fires were frequent and disastrous.

Something had been done to assist rural industries in the struggle with industrial manufactures. Needs previously neglected were being met for the first time, however inadequately.

More spectacular work was done by the zemstvos in the fields of rural medical and veterinary services—which before had scarcely existed—and, above all, in that of elementary education. In 1856, elementary schools in the empire numbered about 8,000. By 1880 the number reached 23,000 in European Russia alone, of which some 18,000 were financed entirely or in part by the zemstvos. In fact, down to the end of Alexander's reign zemstvo or zemstvo-assisted village schools were created at the average rate of 1,000 each year.

The zemstvo school was beginning to occupy the foremost place in Russian primary education. Wherever the zemstvo village schoolmaster appeared, he came as the agent of progress. As such, he had to fight not only the ignorance of the illiterate peasantry but also the distrust of many landowners and the hostility of officials who regarded him as a dangerous propagandist of democratic ideas. However, in the face of every difficulty, the zemstvo teacher made good his position and soon acquired a reputation for his work.

What the zemstvo statute of 1864 did for the Russian villages, the municipal statute of 1870 did for the Russian towns. The area of local self-government was extended by the creation in all towns above a certain size of elective town councils (dumas) analogous in function and status to the district (and in the largest towns the provincial) zemstvos. The dumas suffered from the same restrictions that hampered the full development of the zemstvos: vexatious supervision over key appointments by the provincial Governors; lack of control over the police; an elective system copied from Prussia, but alien to Russian municipal traditions, based on three electoral groups with a few wealthy citizens enrolled in the first, the bulk of the poorer voters in the third. Yet, in spite of these and other difficulties the dumas, like the zemstvos, did much to revive Russian local life. In Moscow and St. Petersburg in particular a whole network of municipal services was created. Municipal or private enterprises were organized to assure the water supply, to provide for the paving and lighting of roads, to run municipal slaughter-houses. The lesser towns also organized municipal services according to their needs. Everywhere the hospitals were improved and increased.

Above all, the dumas, like the zemstvos, devoted their attention to primary education. Usually the dumas formed education committees, charged with the supervision of municipal schools. The results, especially in the capitals, were spectacular. In St. Petersburg, between 1873 and 1880, the number of municipal schools rose from sixteen to eighty-eight, while the amount devoted to education increased from 27,000 roubles in 1871 to ten times that amount in 1881. In Moscow, the development was equally striking, but even in lesser towns like Kiev or Chernigov the educational budget between 1870 and 1880 increased sevenfold and fifteen-fold respectively. "Beyond a doubt", according to one authority, "if at the end of Alexander's reign the Russian towns awaken from the profound slumber into which they were plunged in the reign of Nicholas, it is thanks to the municipal dumas set up by the law of 1870."

The educational achievements of zemstvos and town dumas had been preceded in point of time by a far-reaching liberalization of the educational system under the auspices of the Ministry of Education. This had become particularly marked during the tenure of Golovnin (1861–6), the trusted assistant of the Grand-Duke Constantine. In 1861, the government, along with the liberation of the serfs, had decided to develop elementary education in the villages. The Holy Synod protested against concentrating the development of primary education in the hands of the Ministry, and claimed for the Orthodox priests "the natural preponderance which is their due". Golovnin vigorously opposed the demand and secured the backing of the Tsar. Early in 1862, an imperial decree laid down that only schools opened by the clergy would be controlled by the Synod; the rest would be supervised by the Ministry of Education. It was the indispensable basis for the later educational work of zemstvos and dumas. Secondary education, previously, had been the virtual monopoly of the nobility. A statute of 1864 proclaimed equality for the future. Anyone would be admitted to a secondary school who could pass the entrance examinations. The Ministry did everything in its power to encourage secondary education. The number of schools and the credits for their maintenance increased, as did the salaries of the masters. The teaching was modernized. Prizes were offered for the best text-books on mathematics, science, and modern languages; the translation of foreign works was encouraged. The 'modernization' of Russian secondary education was largely the fruit of Golovnin's labours.

In higher education the Ministry promoted the autonomy of the universities, severely impaired in the days of Nicholas. The university statute of 1863 crowned Golovnin's efforts in this direction. Every university was to be headed by a Rector, elected for four years from among the professors. The administration was entrusted to a council composed of all the professors. This body was responsible for an extensive field, both academic and administrative. It enjoyed complete freedom in the academic sphere, but many appointments continued to require the approval of the Curator of the educational region, a state official attached to each university. A new institution was created, the university tribunal, with authority over the students in matters of discipline. Its president would be the professor of law, whilst the two remaining members would be elected by the council. At the same time, attempts were made to train the future professors. Scholarships for postgraduate study were awarded to promising students; scientific missions abroad were officially encouraged. Thanks to the régime inaugurated by Golovnin, the Russian universities entered a period of rapid development. The period between 1863 and 1880 has been described as "the most brilliant in the history of the Russian universities".

In the spring of 1865 new 'provisional regulations' for the censorship were promulgated; they remained in operation for the next forty years. These regulations marked a further stage in the 'thaw' which, largely owing to Golovnin, had extended to Russian intellectual life. The preliminary censorship was largely, although not wholly, abolished; judicial procedure was substituted for administrative action in dealing with the bulk of press offences. If the legal protection afforded to the Russian press remained incomplete, and if opportunities for arbitrary administrative action remained, the new regulations yet constituted an undeniable improvement. Indeed, if the 'thaw' continued they would offer adequate safeguards for the freedom of the Russian press.

While Golovnin was restoring a measure of freedom to Russian intellectual life, his colleague, D. A. Miliutin, was revolutionizing the administration of the army. Miliutin was described by Bismarck in 1861 as "the most daring and radical spirit among the reformers" and "the bitterest enemy of the nobility", who thought of the future Russia as "a state of peasants, with equality but without freedom . . . somewhat after the model of Napoleon". Already, as a young officer in the Guards Artillery, Miliutin had attracted attention by publishing numerous studies on mathematical and military subjects. Early in 1840 he had seen active service in the Caucasus and been wounded in action against the mountaineers. In 1845 he had been appointed professor at the Military Academy, and during the next fifteen years he published a number of learned works, the best known of which was a study of Suvorov's campaign in 1799. In 1861 he was appointed Minister of War, a post he filled for twenty years. As Minister he continued to maintain close relations with scientific and literary circles, and his friends included the radical professor, Kavelin. He took a lively interest in all social and educational questions. His military reform bears the imprint of his liberal and egalitarian ideas.

Miliutin's first achievement as Minister of War was effectively to reduce the more cruel forms of corporal punishment. The question had been raised in the spring of 1861 in a letter addressed to the Tsar by N. A. Orlov (son of the celebrated 'planter'), the Russian Minister in Brussels. Both Miliutin and the Grand-Duke Constantine, as Minister of Marine, had thrown themselves heart and soul into the struggle. The leading defenders of branding, flogging, and 'spitzruthen' (flogging through the ranks) were the Minister of Justice, Panin, and the Metropolitan Philaret. Their resistance, however, proved unavailing. On his forty-fifth birthday, April 29, 1863, Alexander signed the celebrated ukase abolishing both in the armed forces and for civil prisoners the crueller and more barbarous forms of punishment. Women, except those sentenced to banishment, were exempted from corporal punishment. For men only the milder forms were 'temporarily' retained for certain offences. It was a great humanitarian reform which completely altered the spirit of the Russian army and navy.

Miliutin's tenure of the Ministry of War was marked by a series of enlightened reforms. He began by reducing the term of military service from twenty-five to sixteen years, and by abolishing the more cruel forms of capital punishment. The Military Code was revised and punishments were reduced. The procedure of military courts was modified to bring it more into line with that established for the civil courts in 1864. The practice of using military service as a form of civil punishment was abolished. The condition of the common soldier was improved. At the same time administrative changes improved military efficiency. The obsolescent weapons of the Crimean War were steadily replaced by up-to-date arms and equipment. The command of the troops was decentralized by the setting up of a number of regional commands. The status of the General Staff was raised, and in 1865 the post of Chief of the General Staff was created. Reforms were carried out in the commissariat and the medical services; military engineering was improved, the construction of strategic railways was speeded up. There was hardly a field of military administration that was not touched by the modernizing spirit.

Nowhere was that spirit more noticeable than in the training of future officers. The old Cadet Corps had been fundamentally hostile to any instruction which was not purely military. Moreover, in their military training they had concentrated on routine and formalism, drill and military ceremonial. Miliutin's changes in this field were far-reaching. The Cadet Corps were replaced by army schools (gymnasia), which were organized like their civilian counterparts, only with the addition of their specialist military instruction. Having acquired some general education, pupils then passed to special schools for officer cadets to prepare for service with their chosen branch of the army. Miliutin's reforms thus provided the Russian army with officers who had both a better general education and a better technical training than their predecessors. The new spirit, moreover, did not stop at the schools for future officers. Thanks to Miliutin's efforts, a beginning was made in teaching recruits how to read and write.

Miliutin's main achievement, however, was the introduction of conscription. Under the old system, the obligation of military service rested exclusively on the 'tax-paying orders', that is, the peasants and the lower middle class. From the moment of his appointment, Miliutin urged the abolition of this system of recruiting as incompatible with the emancipation of the serfs. In 1863 a Commission was formed under the Ministry of War to prepare a new statute on military service. The work advanced slowly in the face of bitter opposition. The nobles, still smarting under the 'insult' of 1861, would not hear of their sons being placed on a footing of equality with those of their former serfs. The wealthy merchants were enraged that their wealth should no longer entitle them, as in the past, to buy their sons exemption from military service. Influential Ministers like Tolstoy, Golovnin's successor at the Ministry of Education, and Pahlen, the reactionary Minister of Justice, bitterly opposed the proposals. With the re-action which set in in 1866, a reform in the system of recruiting became, in fact, impracticable.

Plans for reform, however, received a new impetus from the Prussian victories in 1870–1. Under the impact of Moltke's triumphs, a Commission was set up in St. Petersburg to prepare a further measure of military reform. Miliutin drew up a memorandum embodying the principles he hoped to incorporate in it. "The defence of the fatherland", the first article bravely proclaimed, "forms the sacred duty of *every* Russian citizen." The actual call-up would be determined by ballot; only those unfit for service would be exempt. Temporary postponement would be granted in exceptional circumstances on compassionate grounds or in the interests of the national economy. Substitution and exemption by purchase would disappear. Service would continue to be for fifteen years, of which six would be spent with the colours and the rest in the reserve. Miliutin's basic principles were confirmed by Alexander. Many zemstvo assemblies and town dinners, and even a few assemblies of the nobility, presented addresses welcoming the proposals.

No organized opposition against the introduction of conscription developed, but numerous attempts were made during the legislative stages of the measure to secure special privileges and exemptions for a number of different groups. Miliutin, with the support of Alexander, was able to resist most of these demands for special treatment. On January 1, 1874, Alexander signed the statute on military service, conceived wholly in the spirit of the reform. "Under present legislation the duty of military service falls exclusively on the lower class of town dwellers and on the peasants. A significant section of the Russian people is exempt from a duty which should be equally sacred for all. Such an order of things, which came into being in different circumstances, no longer accords with the changed conditions of national life; nor does it satisfy our military needs. Recent events have shown that the strength of armies is based not only on the number of soldiers but on their moral and intellectual qualities. These attain their highest development where the defence of the fatherland has become the common concern of the whole people and where all, without exception and without distinction of calling or estate, combine in this sacred task." The new statute would carry these principles into practice.

Under the new law all young men on reaching the age of twenty became liable to military service. Only three groups were exempted on compassionate grounds, a concession which applied equally to all classes of the population. Each year the number of conscripts required from each military district was chosen by ballot among those liable for service. These recruits had to serve with the colours for six years, after which for nine years they passed into the reserve. Thereafter they were liable for service in a territorial militia until the age of forty. The length of active service was shortened in accordance with educational attainment. Recruits who had completed a higher education served only six months, those with a secondary education two years. Completion of the higher form of elementary schooling, above the level of the village school, reduced active service to three years. Finally, service would be still further reduced for young men who volunteered for service without being drawn by ballot.

The significance of Miliutin's reforms has been summarized by Florinsky : "The new method of conscription was a step towards social equality, even though shorter terms of service for holders of diplomas favoured proprietary groups. The softening of discipline and emphasis on educational activities gave the army an opportunity of contributing to the enlightenment of the masses. Much of the old brutality in the treatment of men by their officers no doubt remained. But the pre-reform army as a penal institution was gone. Men with criminal records were excluded from the forces. Strange as this may seem, it was in the army . . . that Russian democracy scored one of its first modest yet real successes." If Miliutin was able to carry to a successful conclusion his democratic reforms, this was due in no small degree to the Tsar's personal support. Almost since the beginning of his reforming activities, Miliutin had been bitterly criticized by a group of 'old-fashioned' soldiers, who accused him of destroying the army by undermining its discipline and, more justly, of favouring the Staff at the expense of officers in the field. These attacks were inspired by no less a personage than the formidable Field-Marshal Prince Bariatinsky, the popular and self-willed conqueror of the Caucasus. Miliutin, secure in his master's confidence, could afford to ignore criticisms which, in other circumstances, must have put an end to his reforming career.

Like Miliutin, Reutern, the Minister of Finance, was able to carry out important reforms, thanks to Alexander's constant support. Some of the changes introduced by him were of a technical nature. Before 1862 important sources of revenue had been administered independently by various government departments. Reutern for the first time created a unified Treasury and centralized the accounts of all departments in the Ministry of Finance. He improved the methods of audit, and after 1862 the budget was made public. The following year a system of government excise replaced the pernicious system of farming out the sale of spirits.

Of far greater importance than Reutern's technical reforms, however, were his successful efforts to develop the economic life of the empire. The key to Russia's economic progress lay in railway construction, and under Reutern the Ministry of Finance devoted much of its time and resources to the promotion of railway building by private companies. The results achieved were striking. At Alexander's accession the total permanent way of the empire amounted to some 660 miles —of which a considerable proportion was constituted by the Polish section of the line linking Warsaw and Vienna. When Alexander died, the mileage of Russian railways was approximately 14,000. The peak in railway construction occurred between 1868 and 1874. A special effort was made to construct the new lines in a manner to promote the export of Russian grain. The object was fully achieved. Whereas between 1861 and 1865, the average annual export of grain had amounted to some 76 million poods,[1] it had risen for the period 1876–80 to an annual average of 257 million. Along with the economic revival and with the active encouragement of the Ministry of Finance, a great expansion took place in Russian credit institutions. While at the beginning of the reign private banks had hardly existed, the situation was greatly changed between 1863 and 1877. Towards the end of the reign, Russia possessed not only 278 municipal banks but also 33 joint-stock commercial banks. There were 92 societies for mutual credit, and no fewer than 727 loan and savings associations with a total membership of over

[1] One pood equals 36 lb.

200,000. The number of joint-stock companies in the empire had risen to 566, with a total capital (mainly Russian) of over 750 million roubles. The policy of Reutern laid the foundation for a great commercial and industrial development.

The reforms carried out under the auspices of Alexander II thus touched virtually every department of Russian life. Almost everywhere the preponderance of the gentry was reduced, its exclusive privileges cut down or abolished. Everywhere the autonomy of local bodies was increased, the rigid centralization of Nicholas I relaxed. 'Medieval' survivals disappeared from many walks of Russian life. Education and enlightenment assumed a new importance in the zemstvos and dumas, the army and the navy. At the same time railways, credit institutions, better courts, and reformed fiscal and tariff policies laid the foundation for rapid economic development. Russia was ready to turn from a medieval into a modern state.

Yet the undoubted social and economic transformation was uneven and incomplete. Everywhere the institutions of Nicholas continued to exist side by side with those of the reforming age. The Ministry of the Interior controlling the all-important provincial Governors, whose powers were undiminished, remained in the hands of bureaucratic centralizers. The 'self-governing' institutions created by the reforms had little opportunity to develop any real independence. At every step there was unresolved conflict between the new and the old. "The emancipation", writes the French scholar Leroy-Beaulieu, "was followed by numerous reforms, administrative, judicial, military, even financial; yet all these reforms, prepared by different commissions subject to rival or hostile influences, were undertaken in isolation, in an incomplete manner, without coherence and without a definite plan. The task was to build a new Russia; the edifice was constructed upon the old foundations. Building operations were carried out without a blue-print, without a general plan, without an architect to co-ordinate the different operations. By introducing here and there particular innovations while neglecting near-by indispensable repairs; by incorporating everywhere his innovations into the ancient structure, Alexander in the end succeeded after immense labours in making of the new Russia an incomplete and uncomfortable dwelling where friends and opponents of innovation felt almost equally ill at ease."

The task of reconstructing Russia was gigantic; Alexander lacked the firmness, the vision, and the statesmanlike grasp of detail to be completely successful. He showed the same weaknesses in another important field. Nowhere, in fact, was the need for new beginnings more urgent than in Russia's relations with Poland and Finland, the two autonomous states joined to her. Yet in this sphere also Alexander's success, though promising, was—not entirely through his own fault—partial and incomplete.

## Chapter Five

# Alexander, the Poles, and the Finns

THE Poles were among the first to benefit from the
Russian 'thaw'. Early in 1856 Paskievich, the iron
governor of Warsaw, followed Tsar Nicholas to the
grave. His successor, Michael Gorchakov, began, with
the Tsar's full support, to dismantle the system of repression. The crowded prisons emptied, Paskievich's
ubiquitous spies disappeared from public life. The
hated military tribunals ceased to function. An amnesty
allowed *émigrés* as well as Siberian exiles to return to
their native land. In the summer of 1857 a medical
school, widely regarded as the precursor of a restored
Polish university, was opened at Warsaw. The Con-
cordat, a dead letter since its conclusion in 1847, was
put into operation. Finally, the Russian authorities permitted the establishment of the so-called Agricultural
Society. With branches all over Poland, it was nothing
less than a political organization of the Polish nobility
led by Prince Andrew Zamoyski. The Poles, therefore,
had every reason to welcome the accession of Alexander II.

However, the new Tsar would no more sanction any
form of Polish political autonomy than his father after
1831. This, it was held, would simply pave the way for
a demand that the Kingdom should be restored to the
frontiers of 1772. The incorporation in a new Poland
of Russia's western provinces, however, would destroy
the unity of the empire and weaken its strategic position.
Alexander therefore rejected the idea of any autonomy
for the Poles of the Kingdom. During his first visit to

Warsaw as King of Poland, in May 1856, he told Polish notables that he would not change the government of the country. "I will not change anything; what was done by my father was done well. My reign will be a continuation of his." The happiness of Poland depended on "her complete fusion with the peoples of my empire", and the clergy should impress on their parishioners the need for "union with Holy Russia". To curb the political aspirations of the Poles, Alexander twice repeated his celebrated warning against impossible dreams ('*point de rêveries!*'), followed by a distinct threat against those who would not renounce their hopes. Life would be made easier for the Poles, but they must not attempt to sever the political ties uniting them with Russia.

The policy of a 'thaw' within the existing political framework could not satisfy Polish patriots. The leaders of the Polish national movement regarded Gorchakov's mildness as merely an invitation to prepare for a new revolt. Agricultural societies, societies of students and officers arose everywhere and got into touch with each other and with *émigré* committees abroad. The Catholic hierarchy lent its tacit support. Almost unawares the Polish nationalists passed from organization to demonstration. Memorial services were held to commemorate the deaths of Polish national writers. In June 1860 some 20,000 mourners marched to the funeral of the widow of a Polish general killed fighting the Russians in 1831. In November the thirtieth anniversary of the great rising was celebrated, the streets of Warsaw resounding with patriotic hymns. In February 1861 two great demonstrations were organized, during the second of which demonstrators began to skirmish with the police. Russian troops fired on the crowd, killing five and wounding many more.

Faced with mounting tension, Gorchakov tried to avoid all semblance of provocation. Not only all Russian troops but even the police were withdrawn from the streets of Warsaw. A self-appointed 'Delegation' of twelve prominent citizens was permitted to assume responsibility for the maintenance of public order. For forty days it practically ruled Warsaw with the help of a newly formed municipal guard of 2,000 commanded by an Italian, the Marquis Paulucci. The latter assumed his functions amid cheers for Garibaldi and Italy. Delegations similar to that of Warsaw were set up in other Polish towns. The victims of the shooting affray in the capital, regarded as martyrs for their country, received a public funeral. Gorchakov consented to accept an Address to the Tsar from the Agricultural Society, demanding (in somewhat ambiguous terms) the restoration of Polish autonomy. It seemed clear that Russian authority in Poland was disintegrating and that the Tsar's policy of mildness unaccompanied by political concessions was proving a failure.

In face of this situation, opinion at St. Petersburg was divided. In 'liberal' circles there was widespread sympathy for national movements, not only in Poland but in Italy and Hungary as well. It was widely held that concessions to the Poles would bring nearer the day of constitutional changes in Russia itself. Supporters of moderate Pan–Slavism favoured a policy of leniency towards the misguided Polish brothers. At this time there was a widespread readiness among the Russian upper classes to give freedom to the Poles in the Kingdom. Such were the views of some influential personages —the Grand-Duke Constantine and his wife, Alexander Gorchakov, the Foreign Minister, and Valuiev. On the other hand, a strong conservative and military party wished to reassert Russian authority in Poland, if necessary by force of arms. The Tsar now had to choose between putting Poland under martial law and an extension of his policy of concession and reform.

Alexander's first decision on Polish policy was in favour of conciliation. The 'polonophiles' in his entourage had for some time been directing his attention to a wealthy Polish magnate, Alexander Wielopolski. At one time in favour of complete independence for Poland, Wielopolski was now reconciled to working for more limited ends in co-operation with the Tsar. At most he hoped for a return by gradual stages to the constitution of 1815. After a favourable report by Michael Gorchakov, Wielopolski in the spring of 1861 was appointed director of a national Polish commission for religious and educational matters. Following his advice, the Tsar adopted a policy of internal development for Poland. A ukase of March 26, 1861, outlined a programme of reform. Elections would be held in the autumn both for municipal councils and district and provincial assemblies. A Polish Council of State would be set up. Education, under the auspices of Wielopolski's Commission, would be 'polonized'. There would be new Polish secondary schools, and a 'Main School' in Warsaw, a university in all but name. With these concessions Alexander and Wielopolski hoped to reconcile the more conservative and moderate elements in Polish society to a continuance of the Russian connection.

At the same time, Wielopolski was determined to re-establish the authority of the government in the Kingdom. His first act as the virtual ruler of Poland was to close the Agricultural Society. This provoked demonstrations, during which some demonstrators were killed and a number of others injured. The Tsar, on receiving the news, called on Gorchakov, the Viceroy, to take energetic measures. "Please God", he wrote, "that the lesson given to the Warsaw populace on 27 March may have cured it of the desire for similar demonstrations. I insist that at the first sign of their renewal a state of siege should be declared in Warsaw and the Provinces." While Gorchakov, ailing and pacific, was reluctant to aggravate the situation, Wielopolski was disbanding not only the Warsaw 'Delegation' and Paulucci's municipal guard, but also the oppositional Nobles' Club. The result was a further riot, involving loss of life. Alexander now called for energetic action. Gorchakov, unable to stand the strain, fell seriously ill. At the end of May his deputy, a Russian general, was ordered to take over the civil administration of the Kingdom pending the arrival of Sukhozanet, the Minister of War. Sukhozanet, with the help of the Russian garrison, would restore public order and remain in command until the arrival of a new Viceroy, Adjutant-General Count Lambert. The latter, a Roman Catholic personally close to the Tsar, would carry forward the policy of Wielopolski once order had been restored. The Tsar's course, therefore, would be one of firmness in restoring order, accompanied by the grant of the promised reforms.

While Gorchakov lay dying, unrest in Warsaw increased. Demonstrations in the streets, the singing of patriotic hymns in the churches, and masses for the victims of earlier riots were accompanied by daily clashes between populace and police. Sukhozanet reached Warsaw on June 4, five days after Gorchakov's death. Military courts were once again set up. Rioters were banished without trial to the interior of the empire. Order slowly returned to the streets of Warsaw.

Sukhozanet's policy of repression, however, aroused the hostility of Wielopolski. The real ruler of Poland under the aged Gorchakov, the marquis now found himself pushed into the shade by a ruthless Russian soldier. After repeated clashes, he resigned his post in the Polish administration. Alexander, who regretted this, allowed the marquis to send his son to St. Petersburg for personal explanations. The result was an imperial order that Wielopolski should remain at his post pending the arrival of Lambert. Alexander continued to believe in his policy of combining firmness with conciliation.

Lambert reached Warsaw on August 24, and at once fell under Wielopolski's influence. He observed correct legal forms in all his proceedings, encouraged the new administrative autonomy, and showed respect for Polish nationality. Wielopolski was confirmed in his appointment as President of the Commission of Justice and became Vice-President of the State Council. Lambert's mildness, however, was no more successful than Gorchakov's had been. Street processions and the singing of patriotic hymns were resumed. Mounting excitement greeted the news of disorders in Vilna and the declaration of martial law in Lithuania. Alexander wished to impose martial law on the restive parts of Poland. Lambert, prompted by Wielopolski, tried to dissuade him. The Tsar insisted : "For too long already, the agitators have come to count on our forbearance, which they ascribed to weakness and lack of decision. I repeat once again : this state of things must end." On October 11, in the face of continued disorders, Lambert at last declared a state of emergency. Three days later services to commemorate the death of Kosciuszko were held in three Warsaw churches. Russian troops surrounded the churches; two of the congregations refused to leave. On the following morning Russian soldiers entered the churches and made some 1,600 arrests. The Catholic hierarchy in reply closed all churches in the capital. Lambert was in despair. After a violent scene the military commander, General Gerstenzweig, committed suicide. Lambert resigned. Nothing seemed left but a policy of military repression.

Alexander once more had recourse to Sukhozanet, who was again sent to Warsaw with orders "not to permit any illegal acts on any pretext whatever", to sentence the guilty in accordance with the military code and carry out the sentence on the spot. On hearing of Sukhozanet's impending return, Wielopolski resigned. After refusing to listen to the Tsar's appeal to remain at his post, he was summoned to St. Petersburg for explanations. Sukhozanet's severe measures once more restored order, after which he handed over the command to General Luders, Lambert's successor as Viceroy.

Warsaw was now given over to military rule.

Throughout the winter Russian troops bivouacked in the streets of the city. Offenders were tried by military courts; thousands of rifles and other weapons were confiscated; refractory priests were banished to the interior of the empire. Yet at St. Petersburg the party of moderation remained in the ascendant. Constantine continued to smypathize with Wielopolski; Bludov, Gorchakov, and Valuiev still pursued the forlorn hope of winning over Polish 'moderates'. Wielopolski became a much sought after figure in St. Petersburg society. On his advice Felinski, a young professor of the Catholic Academy in St. Petersburg, was appointed to the vacant see of Warsaw. The new archbishop in a conciliatory spirit reopened the closed churches. Wielopolski received permission to visit Warsaw for deliberations in the Council of State on his project for improving the condition of the peasantry. The Tsar, moreover, accepted his recommendation for the complete separation of the civil and military powers in the Kingdom. However, the new head of the civil administration must be a Russian. The Tsar's choice for the post fell on Nicholas Miliutin. The Grand-Duke Constantine opposed the appointment. In his opinion what was needed was 'not a Russian but a Pole'.

Alexander, ever ready to listen to his brother, determined to make a last desperate effort to pacify Poland without further repression. He decided to recall Luders and appoint Constantine in his place. Wielopolski, under the Grand-Duke, would head the civil administration. "The sad conviction", Alexander wrote in the official instructions to his brother, "that all our efforts for the well-being of the Kingdom will never meet the impracticable aims and desires of the extreme patriotic, that is, revolutionary party, must not deflect us from our course." Once again the basic principles of Russian policy were re-stated. The main object would be the restoration of law and order throughout the Kingdom. At the same time, the distinctive institutions of the country would be developed and the reforms either begun or promised would be carried out. Neither a constitution nor a national army was to be thought of, as either of these would amount to a recognition of Polish independence. On the contrary, Poland must always remain, within her present boundaries, an integral part of the Russian empire. Her advanced geographical position made her a bridge between Russia and the rest of Europe.

Alexander's supreme effort at pacification began under unfavourable auspices. Five days before the Grand-Duke's arrival in Warsaw, Luders was seriously wounded by an assassin. Constantine, the day after his arrival, was fired at when leaving the theatre. The following month two attempts were made on the life of Wielopolski. At the same time popular demonstrations continued. In this unpromising situation Constantine and Wielopolski, with a mere handful of supporters, tried to carry out their difficult task of combining repression and reform. The would-be assassins were hanged; Zamoyski was exiled from the Kingdom; Constantine appealed to the Poles to eschew violence and terror. He received generals and merchants, rabbis and artisans. Martial law was lifted in a number of provinces. In August elections were held for some of the new provincial councils. Poles replaced Russians in many official posts; Polish became the language for all official business in the Kingdom. Polish returned to the schools; the 'Main School' at Warsaw was reopened. Jews were relieved of their legal disabilities. A new land law freed the peasants from compulsory labour services.

It was all to no avail. Patriotic demonstrations continued. Secret leaflets called for resistance to the authorities. Collections were started for a rising. Wielopolski, to save his policy, had recourse to an expedient of doubtful legality. A levy of recruits was decreed. The decree—in violation of a law of 1859 prescribing selection by ballot—was phrased in a way to permit the call-up of youths known to be active in the revolutionary movement. In Wielopolski's own words, it was a proscription rather than a conscription. The intentions of the government were betrayed by Polish officials to the revolutionary leaders. When, in January 1863, an attempt was made to execute the plan, only a quarter of the intended conscripts could be apprehended : the rest had fled to the woods. The unsuccessful conscription became the signal, as well as the pretext, for the long-prepared Polish insurrection. The policy of conciliating the conservative elements of Polish society—first followed by Alexander I and later revived by his nephew—had failed irrevocably. Alexander, who for years had sincerely attempted to apply it, was embittered by what he considered Polish ingratitude. Henceforth, he would show little mercy to Polish nationalism, the Polish upper classes, or the Roman Catholic clergy. From now on, he would seek support from the Polish peasantry. He would return to his father's policy of Russification.

Before the new policy could be applied, it was necessary to suppress the insurrection. In spite of great discrepancy in military forces—10,000 inadequately trained and poorly armed Poles against 80,000 Russian regulars—the rising was not finally suppressed until the spring of 1864. The Poles, disunited and ill-led, fought a bitter guerilla war. The Western powers tried to help them by an unavailing diplomatic campaign. At one moment the movement spread, rather ineffectively, into Russia's western provinces, but whereas in the Kingdom the peasants had at least remained passive, those of Lithuania and the Ukraine tended to side with the Russian authorities. After this double failure, the suppression of the insurrection was simply a matter of time.

The Polish rising led inevitably to the abandonment of Wielopolski's policy. In April Constantine was given an assistant, Count Berg, who represented the party of military repression. In June Wielopolski left Poland, a broken man, to spend the rest of his life in disillusionment at Dresden. Michael Muraviev, the reactionary Minister of Domains, became Governor-General of the six north-western provinces with his headquarters at Vilna. Early in September Constantine resigned and was succeeded by Berg. Nicholas Miliutin went to Poland as Secretary of State with Special Functions, accompanied by his Slavophil friends, Samarin and Cherkassky. Cherkassky was appointed head of the civil administration. Soloviev, the friend of the Russian peasants, became head of a Polish department for peasant affairs.

The new men began the double policy of punishing the Polish upper classes and conciliating the peasantry. Muraviev now gained unenviable notoriety as the 'Hangman of Vilna' by his terror against the Poles. The destruction of insurgent bands in Lithuania was followed by mass executions, punitive expeditions, and the wholesale deportation of Polish families to Siberia. Exorbitant fines were imposed on the rebels; some 1,700 estates were confiscated. Severe penalties were imposed for hostile demonstrations, the wearing of mourning, and the use of the Polish language. Punitive action was followed by administrative measures. Catholic monasteries were closed, priests subjected to various restrictions. Conversions to Orthodoxy were encouraged among the Uniat peasants. Orthodox churches were built. Confiscated estates were given to Russian soldiers and officials. Peasant allotments were increased payments reduced by 2 to 16 per cent. redemption payments reduced by 2 to 16 per cent. Orthodox peasants and villagers of Old Believers were generously endowed with land to pay for the better maintenance of Orthodox priests. When Muraviev left Vilna in 1865, he had done much to 'depolonize' Lithuania. The policy was continued by his successor, General Kaufmann.

In the Polish Kingdom a similar pacification was

meanwhile being carried out by Berg. Miliutin and his friends, moreover, were preparing the measure which would strike the death-blow at the dominant position of the Polish gentry. On 19 February/1 March, 1864 (the third anniversary of emancipation in Russia), an imperial ukase endowed the Polish peasants with allotments more generous than those which had been given to their Russian brethren. One-third of all Polish land became the permanent property of the peasants. Unlike their Russian counterparts, the Poles retained the right to use the pastures and some of the woods belonging to their former masters. Woods in which peasants had rights could not be alienated. Peasant land, moreover, could be sold only to peasants. Redemption payments in Poland were less burdensome than in Russia. The peasants merely paid a moderate land tax, levied on *all* land, by means of which the government recouped itself for the sums paid to the landowners in compensation. Administrative arrangements also favoured the peasants. The noble landowners included in the rural communes were often outvoted, on the basis of the size of holdings, by the peasantry. It was the end of a Poland dominated by the gentry and the beginning of her history as a predominantly peasant country.

Miliutin had come to the conclusion that his 'democratic' policy could be carried out only by Russians. In consequence, the remaining Polish institutions were gradually abolished. In 1866 the Kingdom officially lost its name and became the Vistula Region. Its ten provinces were placed under a Russian Governor-General. Administrative amalgamation was accompanied by cultural Russification. Russian became the language of instruction in Polish schools. In 1869 the university of Warsaw was completely russianized. All this was a reversal of Alexander's earlier policies, yet one which circumstances had forced upon him. His wish had been for a slow autonomous evolution of the Kingdom, not for a policy of violent Russification. Similarly he had hoped to work with the moderate nobility and turned to the peasants only as a second choice. As long as was humanly possible, he had persevered in the course recommended by Wielopolski and Constantine. If he had been finally forced to abandon it, this was due almost entirely to the unrealistic dreams and uncompromising line of the Polish patriots and revolutionaries. If the birth of modern Poland was the result of Russian tyranny rather than peaceful Polish evolution, the fault lies not with Alexander but with the Polish nobles who, like the Bourbons, could neither learn nor forget.

The nature of the development Alexander desired for Poland can be seen clearly in his policy towards the Grand-Duchy of Finland. Already, as Tsarevich, he had acquired considerable popularity as Chancellor of Helsingfors University. When, shortly after the conclusion of peace, he paid Finland his first official visit, he was received with enthusiasm. However, as on the occasion of his visit to Warsaw, he struck a warning note. Alluding to the small separatist movement in favour of a return to Sweden, he declared that it was not sufficient merely to be a good Finn. The inhabitants of the duchy must also feel themselves a part of the great empire headed by the Russian Tsar. As in Poland, Alexander outlined a programme of reform. Its main object was to develop the productive forces of the country by the encouragement of trade and the construction of canals and railways. He also promised an extension of elementary education.

The execution of this policy was entrusted to the recently appointed Governor-General, Count Berg, the later Viceroy of Poland. From the beginning Berg showed a sincere concern for the welfare of Finland. In the autumn of 1856, a committee was formed under his presidency to examine the question of communications. Finnish political opinion was divided : conservative officials of the previous reign opposed the construction of railways and wished to develop water communications instead. The liberals favoured a railway linking Helsingfors with the interior. Berg sided with the liberals and helped them to carry the day both in the Senate, the highest administrative body of the Grand-Duchy, and at St. Petersburg. In 1858 work on the line was begun in earnest : it was completed within four years. The railway, combined with new steamship lines on the lakes of the interior, quickened economic life in regions far away from the coast—agriculture in particular benefited from the new developments.

In 1857 Berg chose an assistant in the person of Fabian Langenskiöld, the Governor of Åbo, whom he introduced into the Senate as Minister of Finance. Under their joint ægis efforts were made to develop the country's natural resources. Finnish-speaking agricultural schools were opened. A beginning was made in developing the vast forests of the country. A German expert was invited to advise on them, an Institute of Forestry was opened, a Forestry Service was formed. Saw-mills were freed from fiscal restrictions, and an expansion of the industry followed. In 1860 a credit bank for agriculture was set up; a year later the first private bank. The inequitable Russian tariff on Finnish goods was revised. Finland got her own coinage. Langenskiöld raised a loan in Russia to finance the railway and the currency reform. Guild regulations were relaxed in the backward countryside. They could not, however, be abolished entirely without the Finnish Diet. In this way, during the early years of Alexander's reign, Berg and Langenskiöld laid the foundations of the modern Finnish economy.

But Finnish liberals, like the Polish patriots, wanted more than economic progress. No Finnish Diet had met since 1809, and there was a widespread demand that one should now be called. Administrative as well as political reasons made this desirable. It was more than doubtful whether the new loan for railway construction was constitutional without the approval of the Diet.

And without its participation it was impossible to remove completely the antiquated guild restrictions. Its absence was holding up a number of other reforms. For these reasons even Berg—no friend to elective assemblies—favoured a meeting of the Diet. There had been hopes at the time of Alexander's coronation, but they had been disappointed. During the coronation ceremonies at Helsingfors, the Rector of the university had discoursed on the functions and constitutional importance of the Finnish Diet. His speech was printed and circulated. As severe censorship still prevented all discussion of the 'Diet question', this created a sensation. The Tsar in annoyance gave orders that the Rector should be reprimanded. However, Alexander was soon pacified owing to the intervention of Alexander Armfelt, the Finnish Secretary of State at St. Petersburg. Armfelt, the 'Finnish Wielopolski', enjoyed the Tsar's confidence and was his trusted adviser on the affairs of the duchy. Alexander declared, peaceably enough, that the Rector's unfortunate speech had helped to delay concessions which he wished to make to the Finns. Pressure from below tied his hands, as he had to consider other parts of his empire. Shortly after the incident, Armfelt—against the advice of Berg—secured the reestablishment at St. Petersburg of a Committee on Finnish Affairs, which was joined by two elected representatives of the Finnish Senate.

In the meantime Berg prevented all further discussion of the 'Diet Question'. However, in the interest of his economic reforms, he from time to time made unofficial inquiries at St. Petersburg. The invariable reply was that, while the Tsar's disposition was not unfavourable, a meeting of the Finnish Diet was inopportune on account of possible repercussions in Russia. However, during 1859, Berg won a preliminary success. In response to one of his inquiries the Finnish Senate was asked to draw up a list of matters requiring legislative action. He was not without hope that this might pave the way for an eventual meeting of the Diet.

The Italian national movement was a stimulus to Finnish aspirations. When it was learnt, too, that the first demonstrations in Warsaw had led to an extension of Polish autonomy, the conviction gained ground in Helsingfors that the Diet would soon be called. In the spring of 1861 the Tsar declared that a Diet in Finland would increase unrest among the Poles and aggravate the agrarian situation in Russia. Langenskiöld in reply suggested the formation, as a first instalment, of a 'skeleton' Diet to study legislation on the questions listed by the Senate. Accepting this, the Tsar invited the four Finnish estates (nobility, clergy, townsmen, and peasants) to elect forty-eight representatives, twelve from each estate, to examine matters to be laid before them by the government. They should then submit recommendations on the basis of which 'interim regulations', valid until the next Diet, would be introduced.

The proposal had a mixed reception in Helsingfors, where it was regarded as an attempt to by-pass the Diet. Five liberal Senators invited the Emperor to declare that the new body would only prepare drafts for submission to the next Diet. Radical students organized a demonstration in support of the Senators. Alexander promised that any measures adopted before the meeting of the Diet would be temporary. In the summer the 'Committee' was constituted, but many of its members had made reservations before agreeing to join. Moreover, Finns at St. Petersburg informed the Tsar that the 'Committee' would function only if Berg were replaced as Governor-General. He had made himself unpopular by his high-handed methods, and in November, at his own request, he was relieved of his duties.

Rokossovski, the new Governor-General, of whose qualities the Tsar himself had a low opinion, was well received in Helsingfors. The appointment had been recommended by Armfelt, who knew that his countrymen would welcome a more 'easy-going' representative of Alexander as Grand-Duke. Rokossovski's appointment marked a turning-point in Finnish affairs. Not only did the new Governor relax the censorship so much complained of under Berg, but he made on the Tsar's behalf a formal promise that the Diet would be called when the 'Committee' had completed its task.

The Tsar's promise was repeated more formally in a letter to the President of the 'Committee' early in 1862. By March that body had completed its labours. In July Alexander authorized the drawing up of new standing rules for the proceedings of the Diet. Even the open sympathy for the Poles shown by much of the Finnish press and public did not deflect him from his course. At the height of the Polish crisis in the summer of 1863, an official decree announced that the new Finnish Diet would meet on September 15. At the elections the more moderate elements among the Finns carried the day. In opening the Diet in September, Alexander proclaimed that "in the hands of a wise nation . . . liberal institutions not only are not dangerous but are a guarantee of order and well-being". He added a promise that Diets should be called at regular intervals.

The sessions of the Diet lasted until the following spring. Liberal deputies constantly raised constitutional points, often of a trivial nature. But, apart from this, the Diet did much to promote the well-being of Finland. Money was voted for elementary education, railway construction, and currency reform. Provision was made for extending village self-government. Laws safeguarding freedom of publication were drafted. The National Bank was placed under the control of the Estates. Alexander was irritated by the aggressive spirit shown by some of the deputies and saw less the solid achievement than the ingratitude of the critics. His closing speech, read in Russian by Rokossovski, was blunt, and concentrated on listing the advantages derived by Finland from her association with Russia.

Yet Alexander's irritation involved no change of policy. Throughout the years which followed the Finnish constitution was scrupulously observed. Diets, called at regular intervals, were enabled to develop Finnish autonomy. In 1865 the Senate decreed that after the first day of 1872 all officials in the duchy must use only the Finnish language. A law introduced in 1869 ended church control over schools, while at the same time reducing the power of the state in Church affairs. In 1874 a reformed conscription law was introduced. Three years later Finland adopted the gold standard.

In this manner, in the reign of Alexander II and sometimes with his personal participation, the foundations of modern Finland were laid. To the Finns, his assassination in 1881 was an occasion of sincere regret and grief. To this day, while other relics of Russian rule have long since vanished from Finland, the statue of the 'Tsar Liberator' dominates the Senate Square in the heart of official Helsinki.

Alexander, therefore, may be regarded as the father of modern Finland as well as of modern Poland. In both countries he endeavoured to pursue a policy of reform and gradual progress towards increasing autonomy. The Poles did not, indeed could not, respond to this approach; the Finns, in spite of a widespread desire for speedier evolution, had the good sense and statesmanship to content themselves with the possible. Wielopolski's policy ended in disaster, that of Armfelt in modest success. Alexander, in Poland and in Finland, pursued his course with tenacity in the face of disappointments and provocation. Ignoring the attacks of Russian nationalists who blamed him for going too far and of radicals who considered his progress too slow, he followed steadfastly the path of reform combined with the maintenance of order and authority. Provided the unity of the empire was maintained—and it is difficult to blame an emperor of Russia for making this proviso —Alexander was eager to promote the well-being of his 'satellite' subjects. In Poland and Finland, as in the rest of the empire, his policy was one of moderate reform and 'modernization'.

## Chapter Six

# The Tsar Despot

IN the empire proper, as in Poland and Finland, Alexander soon experienced the difficulties inseparable from a 'thaw' accompanied by major reforms. The relaxation of the reins of government following thirty years of Nicholas's stern regime was naturally accompanied by a decline in the imperial authority. A public without political sense or experience, rigidly debarred for decades from all share in public affairs, took advantage of freer conditions to criticize with complete irresponsibility every measure of the Emperor and his government. Again, the modest extension of freedom permitted by the new Tsar inevitably produced a pressing demand for more. Restraints accepted almost without murmur under Nicholas were suddenly felt to be irksome; the public, hitherto largely excluded from state affairs, now protested that the relative freedom given by Alexander was inadequate. Finally, any reform, and in particular one as far-reaching as the liberation of the serfs, must of necessity be a compromise affronting vested interests while disappointing those who had expected more. The liberation as well as his other measures earned the reforming Tsar not gratitude but widespread criticism and hostility. Signs of discontent appeared among all groups of the population. By 1862 Russia apparently was drifting into chaos.

The ferment first began to assume serious proportions shortly after the liberation of the serfs. The trouble—as so often in periods of 'thaw'—started in the higher educational institutions. Student disorders on minor points

of discipline began in Kiev in 1857, and subsequently
spread to Moscow and other universities. Alexander
directed that these first breaches of discipline should be
overlooked, but his leniency merely helped to encourage
the disorders. Both Polish and socialist influences came to
play a part in the unrest. Some professors sympathized
with socialist ideas and were subscribers to Herzen's
revolutionary publications. From the safety of London,
Herzen was preaching fraternization between Russian
radicals and Polish patriots. His plea was not without
effect. In February 1861 the funeral of the Ukrainian
poet Shevchenko was followed by a Requiem Mass for
the first victims in Poland. Three hundred Russian
students and several professors attended the service held
at St. Petersburg in a Roman Catholic church. At a
similar service in Moscow, a Russian student declared
that Russians and Poles had a common enemy—the
Russian government. Polish students in return joined in
demonstrations organized by their Russian fellows. The
most extensive of these followed the 'massacre of
Bezdna', where Russian troops had fired on unarmed
peasants. At the same time socialist propaganda was
flooding the military schools from the Corps of Pages to
the Artillery Academy, where Professor Lavrov combined mathematical instruction with the advocacy of
social revolution.

In July *Velikoruss* (The Great Russian), the first of
a series of illegal proclamations, began to circulate in
St. Petersburg. It was an appeal to the 'educated classes'
(whatever the term might mean) to take power from the
hands of the incompetent government. The mistakes of
the Tsar and his advisers were driving the peasantry to
revolt (this was an echo of Bezdna); they would in time
provoke another Pugachev rising. Early in September a
second issue of *Velikoruss* repeated the earlier warning
and called on the educated classes to demand a constituent assembly to reorganize the country. A third
issue, some weeks later, gave the text of a proposed

Address to the Tsar. About the same time an appeal *To the Younger Generation* made its appearance, which called for a constitution and a social transformation. Russia should pass directly from a semi-feudal into a socialist state. The manifestoes created an impression : there was a widespread feeling in St. Petersburg that revolution was approaching.

In the spring of 1861 the Council of Ministers debated the state of the universities. Some Ministers wished to close all universities 'for reorganization'. The Tsar rejected the suggestion, but accepted the resignation of Kovalevsky, the liberal Minister of Education. He was replaced by Admiral Putiatin, a rigid disciplinarian. The new Minister put new university regulations into force at the opening of the academic year (early in October). The students of St. Petersburg organized a protest meeting in one of the lecture halls. By order of the authorities, all lectures were suspended and the university was closed. The students assembled in the courtyard and marched, as a body, to the house of the Curator. The police arrested the ringleaders—which produced another mass meeting. The Governor-General called out troops, and the meeting dispersed. Some days later the students organized another meeting; thirty-five were arrested. Another time troops were called out and scuffles developed between them and the students. Some three hundred students were taken to the fortress of SS. Peter and Paul. On the same day the students of Moscow staged a demonstration. These demonstrations found an echo in every institution of higher education in the empire.

When matters had come to this pass, the Tsar intervened in person. Hurrying back to St. Petersburg, he expressed dissatisfaction at the clumsiness of the authorities. He disapproved of the imprisonment of the students. The Governor-General was relieved of his duties and replaced by the humane Prince Suvorov. However, the university was to remain closed until a new statute for all Russian universities had been completed. Funds were placed at the disposal of Suvorov to help needy students forced to move to other universities. The ringleaders among the students were banished to distant provinces to live under police supervision. Soon afterwards, Putiatin's place was taken by the liberal Golovnin.

The 'settlement' of the student problem did little to reduce the general ferment. The demonstrations in the streets of Warsaw were assuming alarming proportions. Moreover, subversion was beginning to affect the Russian army. Late in 1861 a foreign observer noted: "From general to major, all are reliable but of limited intelligence; from major to sergeant-major, all are unreliable. The common soldier is unpredictable and will follow whoever influences him." In May 1862 four junior officers were arrested in Warsaw, together with two non-commissioned officers. Two further officers absconded. A commission of inquiry discovered that two more officers were involved. All were charged with having circulated among the lower ranks "lying and impertinent slanders about the emperor and the ruling dynasty", and with having read and passed to them "books and pamphlets of a subversive nature (*Velikoruss*, *The Bell*, the *Historical Almanack*) with the object of undermining their loyalty and obedience to the lawful authorities". Of the accused, three were sentenced to death, one (an N.C.O.) to flogging through a double row of soldiers. If he survived (which was doubtful) he would serve twelve years' hard labour in the mines. On July 28 the sentences were carried out in the Polish fortress of Modlin.

Even more alarming to the authorities were certain developments in another sphere. In May 1862 there circulated in St. Petersburg another clandestine leaflet, the most violent of them all. *Young Russia* demanded not only elective national and provincial assemblies as well as elected judges, but also publicly owned factories, the dissolution of monasteries, universal education, and the abolition of marriage. The object of the recommended changes was to "change radically and without exception all the foundations of contemporary society". The ruling classes would resist; the people must pitilessly strike them down. Some weeks after the appearance of *Young Russia*, a series of devastating fires broke out all over Russia. In St. Petersburg itself a week of outbreaks culminated in a conflagration which gutted two thousand shops and warehouses. "If there had been wind on that day, half the city would have perished in the flames." There was evidence to suggest that the fires were started deliberately. Those guilty were never discovered, but public opinion attributed the outbreaks to Poles and socialists—who, in their turn, asserted that the fires were started by right-wing *agents provocateurs*. Whoever was responsible, the fires greatly increased the prevailing feeling of insecurity and alarm.

The unrest of 1861-2 which ended the honeymoon of Alexander's reign profoundly affected the Tsar's temperament and outlook. In the first place, his health was beginning to be affected. Already in 1860 he had returned from a visit to Warsaw in a state of near-prostration which led foreign diplomats to speculate whether he might not be suffering from tuberculosis. By 1862 his nerves were on edge. In a letter to the Grand-Duke Constantine he dwelt on the need to attain calmness of spirit in the face of daily disturbing rumours. "Unhappily I know from my own experience that this is difficult; I am often seized by an internal trembling when particularly stirred by anything. But one must control oneself, and I find prayer the best means to this end." An instance of Alexander's loss of control is recorded by one of his pages. It was on the day before the disloyal officers were shot at Modlin. The Tsar had given a final examination to cadets about to be commissioned. At the end of the parade he called together the newly commissioned officers. On horseback, he congratulated them quietly and said a few words about military duty and loyalty. Then, changing his tone, "distinctly shouting out every word, his face suddenly distorted with anger", he continued : "But if anyone among you—from which God preserve you—should prove himself in any circumstances disloyal to the Tsar, the throne, and the fatherland—take heed of what I say —he will be treated with the full se-ve-ri-ty of the law without the slightest com-mi-ser-a-tion!" His voice failed. With an expression of blind rage on his face, he violently spurred his horse and galloped away. Yet at other moments his page was struck by "that problematic, absent-minded gaze, which I had often begun to notice".

Alexander's anger found expression in the policy of his government. In September 1861 Mikhailov, a poet, was arrested as the reputed author of one of the clandestine handbills. He was tried and sentenced to penal servitude in Siberia, where he died four years later. This was the first political trial since the days of Nicholas, a landmark in the history of Alexander's reign. The great fires provoked further repressive action. The leading radical journals were suspended for eight months. Chernyshevsky, the editor of one of them, was arrested together with some other journalists. Detained for two years, he was finally brought to trial and sentenced—on inconclusive evidence—to fourteen years of hard labour in the Siberian mines and exile for the rest of his life. In the meantime, a special Commission had been set up in the Third Division to unearth the authors of illegal leaflets and members of secret revolutionary organizations. The Tsar himself based high hopes on the results of this Commission; its discoveries were negligible. It did, however, report that the Sunday-school movement (classes run by students and journalists for artisans and workers), which had greatly developed in the last two years, was dangerous. All Sunday schools were closed. Such was the beginning of the duel to the death between Alexander II and the Russian revolutionary movement.

The first round in the struggle went decisively in favour of the Tsar and his Ministers. The great fires produced a change in Russian public opinion. That part of society at St. Petersburg, and especially at Moscow, "which carried most weight with the government, suddenly threw off its liberal garb, and turned not only against the most advanced section of the reform party but even against its moderate wing". The Polish insurrection completed the conversion. Herzen's stand in favour of the Poles cost him the support of all patriots among the Russian reformers; the circulation and influence of *The Bell* rapidly declined. Herzen's loss was the gain of Michael Katkov, a 'repentant liberal', who now stood forth as the champion of Great Russian nationalism. From this moment his *Moscow Gazette* replaced Herzen's paper as the mouthpiece of Russian opinion. Western diplomatic intervention fanned Russian patriotism to fever heat. Gorchakov, by expressing popular opinion with uncompromising firmness, became the hero of the hour. Nationalism rather than radicalism had become the fashionable creed.

The temporary eclipse of Russian radicalism did not, however, put an end to the Tsar's anxieties. His struggle with the radical intelligentsia appeared, for the moment, won; that with the upper classes was continuing without respite. Constitutional demands were not confined to the Poles and Finns but were voiced with increasing insistence among the Russians themselves. As early as 1859 the delegates sent to St. Petersburg by the provincial committees on liberation had demanded a national assembly. Oligarchs who desired to increase the influence of the nobility and genuine believers in constitutionalism alike supported the movement. It possessed the sympathy of Valuiev, who wrote : "On 19 February [the day of liberation], the sun of imperial favour warmed the bottoms of the

131

valleys; now it must illumine and warm the summits and the slopes."

The spearhead of the constitutionalists had lain at first in the assemblies of nobility. At the turn of 1861. several of these had discussed general political questions. At St. Petersburg a proposal calling for a national assembly with advisory functions was defeated by only two votes. In Moscow and Tula similar demands were raised. More drastic was the action of thirteen noblemen of Tver, all of whom had taken part in putting the liberation statute into effect. In an address to the Tsar, after criticizing in undiplomatic language the defects of the statute, they called for a national assembly representing the whole Russian people. The Address was printed and circulated in the countryside; it was even read at village meetings. The Tsar—against the advice of Valuiev—decided to make an example. After a sojourn in the fortress of SS. Peter and Paul, the signatories appeared before a special court, which condemned them to detention in a lunatic asylum and the loss of civil rights. The first part of the sentence was carried out for four days, the second proved permanent.

Alexander's views on the problem of a constitution were expounded in conversation with Bismarck late in 1861. The idea of receiving advice from subjects other than his officials, the Tsar explained, was not in itself objectionable. Greater participation in public affairs by respectable notables could only be an advantage. The difficulty was that it had never in practice been possible to stop liberal development at an appropriate point. This would be particularly true in a country like Russia, where the indispensable political sense and training were confined to a narrow circle. Constitutionalism was not in accord with Russia's political tradition. Throughout the interior of the empire common people still regarded the monarch as their 'paternal and absolute God-given ruler'. This sentiment, which amounted to a religious belief, was quite independent of any personal attachment. The veneration with which the Russian people surrounded the throne of its emperors could not be shared. To call representatives of the nobility or the nation to share his absolute power would be to diminish, without compensating gain, the authority of the government. In particular, God alone knew what would become of relations between landowners and peasants if the imperial power was no longer strong enough to exercise a dominating influence. Views like these were not without foundation; they forbade major concessions to the constitutionalists.

After the pacification of Poland the constitutional movement received a new impetus from the newly created zemstvos. In December 1865 the zemstvo of St. Petersburg demanded the creation of a central zemstvo office; the following year the demand was repeated with even greater insistence. Alexander felt unable to give up his autocratic power. He explained his reasons during a paternal talk with one of the constitutionalists. "And now", said the emperor, "I suppose you consider that I refuse to give up any of my powers from motives of petty ambition. I give you my imperial word that, this very minute, at this very table, I would sign any constitution you like, if I felt that this would be for the good of Russia. But I know that, were I to do so to-day, to-morrow Russia would fall to pieces." There can be little doubt that the Tsar was sincere in his belief. Considering the interest of Russia to be at stake, he decided to act after the second demand of the St. Petersburg zemstvo. The assembly was dissolved, and several of its more prominent members were exiled. The constitutional movement of the zemstvos died down and did not revive until 1875.

The suppression of the St. Petersburg zemstvo was only part of a wider policy following the first attempt on Alexander's life. On April 16, 1866, while taking his daily walk in the Winter Garden in the capital, he was fired on and saved only by the prompt action of a bystander (a *muzhik*). The would-be assassin turned out to be Karakozov, a member of the lesser nobility, expelled from Kazan university. A special Commission under Muraviev, the 'Hangman of Vilna', was set up at once to investigate the attempt. Little was discovered, but Muraviev was forced to admit that in that very social group—including the government itself—there were individuals who wished to overthrow the monarchy. Karakozov was hanged; thirty-four members of secret groups suffered lesser penalties; numerous innocent people were arrested.

Muraviev's report drew attention to the fact that many members of revolutionary circles were students. This was attributed to the state of Russian education. Teachers at all levels were politically unreliable; insubordination was rife in the schools as in the universities. The younger generation was steeped in atheism, materialism, and socialism, inculcated not only by the teachers but also by the radical 'progressive' press. Impressed by this report, the Tsar resolved to change the spirit of Russian youth. A Rescript to the President of the Council of Ministers called for the suppression of subversive activities in all educational establishments. Golovnin was forced to resign and replaced by D. A. Tolstoy, the obscurantist Procurator of the Holy Synod. Katkov bitterly attacked the nihilism of the younger generation. His educational ideal was the 'gentleman' produced by English public schools. He agreed with Tolstoy that the harmful spirit among the young sprang from the teaching of science, which produced a superficial, materialistic outlook. He objected also to the manner of teaching history and Russian literature, both of which were largely in the hands of liberals. The remedies against the 'bad spirit' were to be found in discipline, inculcated through Greek, Latin, and mathematics.

In the teeth of fierce opposition in the Imperial Council, Tolstoy and Katkov 'reformed' the educational system. The teaching of science was excluded from 'grammar schools', that of other 'suspect' subjects reduced. Ancient languages, with a heavy emphasis on grammar, received pride of place. Teachers became officials and were forced to act as spies and policemen. Under the mask of strict obedience, hypocrisy and time-serving were encouraged. Moreover, thousands of pupils failed to pass the new severe examinations in classics and had to leave the schools without diplomas. Many others were excluded from schools and universities for trivial breaches of discipline and went to swell the ranks of the malcontents. The excluded student would soon become the most typical figure in the ranks of the revolutionaries. An ultra-conservative Russian publicist noted that Tolstoy had created dozens and even hundreds of secondary schools, but his system— even more than that of his liberal predecessor—had made them into 'hotbeds of political subversion'.

The educational sphere was not the only one affected by Karakozov's shot. Immediately after the attempt the aged chief of the Third Division tearfully offered his resignation and proposed as his successor Peter Shuvalov, his former chief of staff. Shuvalov's first act after his appointment was to demand the replacement of Annenkov, the chief of the St. Petersburg police. Annenkov was a protégé of Suvorov, the liberal Governor-General of the city. A fierce struggle began between the 'new men' and the surviving 'liberals' for the body and soul of the Tsar. The weak emperor became the central figure in an incident which, in his father's time, would have been unthinkable.

On hearing Shuvalov's demand, Suvorov rushed to the Tsar and declared that, without Annenkov, he could not answer for the security of the capital. Alexander agreed with Suvorov. Egged on by Shuvalov, Berg, the Governor-General of Poland, recommended General Trepov, the chief of police in Warsaw, for a similar appointment in St. Petersburg. Alexander promptly offered Trepov Annenkov's place. Trepov accepted on condition that he should not be responsible to the Governor-General but report directly to the Tsar. (This was the Russian equivalent to a seat in the Cabinet.) Alexander declared angrily that he would not accept such terms: Trepov must accept the post as it was. The general had the courage—some might say the impertinence—to reply : "At your Majesty's command. Your orders will be carried out, but I must warn your Majesty that I cannot accept responsibility for the safety of St. Petersburg. That responsibility must remain with the Governor-General." The Tsar did not have Trepov arrested—as his father would certainly have done.

Trepov at once went to Suvorov to report his conversation with the Emperor. Suvorov threatened to repay him. Shuvalov now decided to destroy the inconvenient Governor-General. Three times he represented to the Emperor that in the interest of public order the office of Governor-General of St. Petersburg must be abolished. Alexander replied : "I am ready to do anything, but this, never !" At Shuvalov's fourth attempt the Tsar gave ear without signs of irritation. A few days later, at a hunting party, he informed Suvorov of his decision to abolish the post of Governor-General. After the interview Suvorov pointedly declared that he would retire to the estate where his grandfather, the great Suvorov, had lived in exile under the tyrant Paul. "Trepov", a conservative nobleman recorded, "became the unchallenged ruler of St. Petersburg, and people began to breathe more freely under his firm yet intelligent administration."

During a visit to Paris in the summer of 1867, the Tsar was fired at again, this time by a Pole named Berezowski. This second attempt finally established the ascendancy of Shuvalov. The Chief of Police had the manners of a gentleman (always an important point with Alexander II) and combined ability with tact.

Shuvalov alone could give the harried Tsar a feeling of calm, security and confidence. He became indispensable to his master, and soon enjoyed the reputation of being all-powerful in domestic affairs. On his advice, the Ministries of Justice and the Interior were handed over to conservatives. In 1867 Zamiatnin, the patron of the judicial reforms, made way for Count Pahlen, a reincarnation of the late Panin. The following year Valuiev fell victim to an unscrupulous intrigue mounted against him by the Tsarevich (the future Alexander III, advised by his ultra-conservative tutor, Pobedonostsev) with the enthusiastic support of Katkov. With the transfer of his Ministry to General Timashev, the establishment of the reactionary régime was complete.

The Tsar, under the impression of two attempts on his life, resigned himself to police rule. Personally brave, he had not flinched under the fire of Berezowski, but his peace of mind was disturbed. If Trepov now appeared at the palace with his daily report a few minutes after the appointed time, he was met with the anxious question whether all was quiet in the city. Indeed, Alexander had become almost a prisoner of the police. Kropotkin records how, one day, a senior official of the Third Division repeated in a private house a conversation in which the Emperor had reprimanded a member of the imperial family. Asked how he could know the details, the policeman replied: "The words and opinions of his Majesty must be known to our department. How else could a delicate institution like the state-police be managed? Be assured that the Emperor is the most closely watched person in all St. Petersburg."

By this time Shuvalov's police were much concerned with the Emperor's private affairs. During 1865 the Tsar, a connoisseur of female charms, had developed a passion for a young aristocratic girl, Catherine Dolgoruky, then eighteen years of age. The following summer she became his mistress. Alexander, in his delight, made a solemn promise: "To-day, alas", he declared, "I am not free; but, at the first opportunity, I will marry you; for from now onwards and for ever I regard you as my wife before God." In the autumn, the liaison became regularly established. Three or four times a week, the princess would come secretly to the Winter Palace. Through a low door, of which she had the key, she would make her way to a secluded room on the ground floor. The connection was soon known in St. Petersburg society. Relatives hurried Catherine to Naples. The two lovers wrote to each other every day. They met again in Paris during Alexander's visit. After his return to St. Petersburg, Catherine was established in a luxurious flat. Appearances were preserved—but with increasing difficulty. The need to maintain at least a pretence of secrecy subjected Alexander to increasing personal strain; it multiplied the responsibilities of those charged with his protection.

In May 1872, Catherine bore Alexander a son, christened George; other children followed. The event caused indignation in the imperial family and in aristocratic circles in the two capitals. A romantic liaison had been accepted; it was different when the matter became a public scandal. There was indignation that a ruler of fifty-four, already a grandfather, should thus lower the prestige of the dynasty. The disparity in the ages of the lovers caused comment. More serious, the health of the Empress was known to be failing. Would Catherine Dolgoruky be one day legitimate wife, consort, empress? Might not even the order of succession be imperilled? Filled with anxiety and foreboding, Russian society rallied behind the heir-apparent and his wife. The future Alexander III abhorred moral laxity and soon became the bitter enemy of Catherine and her friends. The female members of the imperial family shared his indignation. Alexander's liaison with Princess Dolgoruky had become a matter of public concern. It finally alienated from the Tsar the respect of Russian society, destroyed his moral prestige, and split the imperial family.

Moreover, it was not long before Princess Dolgoruky began to exercise a political influence. At first she had been simply a sympathetic listener, offering her lover opportunities to unburden himself of the cares of state. Inevitably, however, she became the rallying-point for a group opposed to the conservatives and the Tsarevich. Like the heroine of Tolstoy's *Anna Karenina,* her equivocal position forced upon her a life of semi-seclusion. Both Catherine and Alexander, therefore, were more than grateful to those who, disregarding a strict official boycott, were willing to join in the couple's modest social life. These, apart from the Tsar's closest friend, Sasha Adlerberg, came to include some men of 'liberal' views—Valuiev, steadily returning to favour; Abaza, a future Minister of Finance, and, later, Count Loris-Melikov.

Among those who refused to pay court to Catherine Dolgoruky was Peter Shuvalov, the all-powerful chief of police. Some of his remarks—duly reported in the highest spheres—were far from favourable to the princess. Finally, he had the unwisdom to oppose some of her friends in a doubtful railway speculation. In 1874 Shuvalov—against his wishes—was suddenly appointed ambassador in London. He was replaced by Potapov, a nonentity. The results of his disappearance were not long in showing themselves. The efficiency of the police organization deteriorated. Soon the government would enter—with weakened forces—its mortal combat with the revolutionary movement. The infatuation for Catherine Dolgoruky was closely connected with the decline in the Tsar's authority and his inability to curb effectively the dangerous influences at work in Russian society.

## Chapter Seven

# Alexander II
# and the Russian Expansionists

IT is in the field of foreign policy that in the later
years of the reign, Alexander's inability to control the
more explosive forces in Russian society is most clearly
revealed. In his dealings with the representatives of
Russian expansion, he showed in the fullest measure the
ambiguity and weakness characteristic of so many of
his undertakings. Alexander's approach to problems of
foreign policy had been fundamentally one of caution,
based on an overriding desire to preserve peace. The
reasons for this were not primarily humanitarian.
Russia after the Crimean War clearly needed a prolonged period of recuperation, and no one understood
this better than the Tsar. Soon a second imperative
reason had been added. The Austro-French war of 1859
—originally encouraged by Russia—was seen before
long to have opened the floodgates of revolutionary
nationalism. The risings in central Italy, followed by
Garibaldi's famous expedition, stimulated national
movements in Germany, Hungary, Denmark, and
Poland. Moreover, Napoleon III in 1863 showed an unmistakable desire to intervene on the side of the insurgent Poles. Any war in Europe threatened to produce results unwelcome to the Russian government.

The resurgence of the revolutionary tide during 1860
suggested to the Tsar not only closer relations with
Prussia but even a measure of reconciliation with 'per-

fidious' Austria. The British government, estranged from France after the Polish crisis of 1863, seemed inclined to associate itself with a conservative defensive grouping. Such a system, dear to the heart of Alexander and Gorchakov, demanded the preservation of peace in Europe. Miliutin and Reutern, in the interest of their military and financial reforms, strongly supported a cautious and pacific diplomacy. In pursuit of this policy, the Russian government went to the length of repeatedly warning the Balkan Christians against 'premature' insurrections. Russia, during the period of her transformation, must preserve friendly relations with both England and Austria; she must not give cause for alarm in either Central Asia or the Balkans. Such, in brief, was the official policy of Alexander II and Gorchakov.

This policy of caution failed to satisfy important expansionist forces in Russian society. It was precisely during the reign of Alexander II that Russian imperialism assumed a 'modern' form. The bearers of the new imperialism were, in the first place, energetic and ambitious proconsuls in the outlying portions of the empire. They were supported by colonial soldiers eager for fame and booty. Indeed, the desire for conquest was well-nigh universal among the military forces stationed in 'colonial' territories. A contemporary Russian observer noted : "A positive fever for further conquest raged among our troops—an ailment to cure which no method of treatment was effective, especially as the correctives applied were frequently interspersed with such stimulants as honours and decorations. Not only the Russian Generals but even the youngest Lieutenants craved after further extension of territory, while those of the officers who were entrusted with any sort of independent command carried into effect their individual schemes. It was, indeed, impossible that such desires should be resisted when by gratifying them it was possible for a Lieutenant in four years to become a General."[1]

Military ambition was reinforced by commercial aspirations. "Almost hand in hand with the conquering generals", writes B. H. Sumner, "went the Khludovs, Moscow textile millionaires, Pervushin with his lead mines, Kolesnikov with his gold and coal scandals . . . and the big trading firms of Pupyshev and Bykovsky."[2] In 1876, the Governor of Transcaspia noted that recently the eastern shores of the Caspian had attracted attention from capitalists and various big companies. He was approached on all sides with applications for concessions for fishing, salt, sulphur, and oil. A high-placed court official headed a particularly important salt company. The military and commercial interests favouring expansion were not without support in official circles. The influential Asiatic Department of the Ministry of Foreign Affairs looked with favour on a policy which might easily come into conflict with that adopted by Alexander and Gorchakov.

The Tsar's attitude towards the movement for expansion had been from the start ambiguous. While favouring caution and restraint, he yet delighted in any extension of Russian territory and influence. Already in 1850 he had sided with 'imperialism' when supporting the annexation of the Amur region in opposition to Nesselrode, the Foreign Minister. Nicholas Muraviev, the celebrated Governor-General of Eastern Siberia (1847–61) came to St. Petersburg to fight in person the Ministers who vetoed Far Eastern expansion in order to avoid clashes with China and Great Britain. It was the Tsarevich's personal intervention that had turned the scales in his favour. Muraviev left St. Petersburg with authority to extend the area of Russian occupation. The fruits of the new policy were seen in the foundation of

[1] Quoted in B. H. Sumner, *Russia and the Balkans 1870–1880*, (O.U.P., 1937), p. 48.
[2] Ibid., p. 46.

Vladivostok (July 1860) and the signing of the Treaty of Pekin, negotiated at the same time by Colonel Ignatiev (the future Pan-Slav leader). By that treaty China finally ceded the regions of the rivers Amur and Ussuri, which became the Russian Maritime Province. Thanks in no small degree to Alexander's support, a great new province had been added to the Russian empire.

The Tsar gave similar encouragement to colonial expansion in the region of the Caucasus. In this instance it was a question of completing a conquest begun many years before. In 1857 Prince Bariatinsky had been appointed Viceroy at Tiflis with orders to complete the subjugation of the area. After two years of heroic resistance Shamil, the leader of the mountaineers of the eastern Caucasus, had been forced to surrender to the Russians. Thereafter had come the turn of the proud Circassians defending their mountain fastnesses above the Black Sea. By 1864 they also were subdued, and those who would not accept Russian rule had migrated to the territories of the Sultan of Turkey. The Caucasus was firmly in Russian hands.

The conquest of the Caucasus left large Russian armies unemployed and longing for further action. Under Alexander's brother, the Grand-Duke Michael (Bariatinsky's successor as Viceroy), Russian forces began to cross the Caspian and to advance southwards along its eastern shores towards northern Persia. In 1869 the important base of Krasnovodsk was established 150 miles from Baku across the Caspian Sea. In 1874, under the control of headquarters in Tiflis, an elaborate Trans-Caspian Military District was established. Its creation had been preceded by one of the periodic clashes between the colonial proconsuls and the civil authorities at St. Petersburg. Gorchakov and Reutern, fearing political complications with Great Britain, opposed expansion in this area. The Grand-Duke Michael, supported by Miliutin, persuaded the Tsar to sanction the move. As on other occasions, Alexander finally gave his vote in favour of expansion. Once the new command was set up, the 'Caucasians' began to press forward towards Merv and the Afghan border. In 1879 army engineers began work on the Trans-Caspian Railway along the northern frontier of Persia. Relentlessly, the Russians were advancing into the area of ill-defined border territories with Persia and Afghanistan.

In the meantime, other Russian forces were advancing further to the east. In 1864, virtually on his own initiative, Colonel (later General) Cherniaev captured the cities of Turkestan and Chimkent. The following year he took the important city of Tashkent, provoking an armed conflict with the Amir of Bokhara. The Russians occupied part of his territory. In 1866 the extensive territories seized by Russia since 1847 were formed into the Governor-Generalship of Turkestan. General Kaufmann, one of Russia's great empire-builders, became its first ruler. During his proconsulship (1867–83), the conquest of Central Asia was completed. A protégé of Miliutin, Kaufmann had from the start enjoyed full political and diplomatic powers for dealing with the independent states of Central Asia. Under his direction operations against the khanates of Kokand and Bokhara were prosecuted with vigour. In 1868 the key cities of Bokhara and Samarkand fell to the Russians. Kokand and Bokhara became Russian vassal states. In 1873 Khiva, the last independent khanate, acknowledged Russian suzerainty. This was followed by the subjugation of the independent Turcomans and a rapid advance towards Herat and Afghanistan.

The Russian expansion in Central Asia raised the question of a possible clash with Great Britain. The alarm felt by British administrators in India was beginning to communicate itself to the home government and British public opinion. Repeated inquiries from London forced the Tsar and Gorchakov to recognize the international implications of the Russian advance in Asia. Alexander was faced with a dilemma. At heart an expansionist, he appreciated that failure to respect British susceptibilities might in certain circumstances provoke an anti-Russian coalition. He therefore resolved to restrain the colonial hotheads and calm British apprehensions.

In a lengthy circular of November 1864, Gorchakov tried to justify the Russian advance in Central Asia. The needs of security and the interests of trade, he argued, compel any major state bordering on areas occupied by warlike tribesmen to bring them under its control. "The United States in America, France in Africa, Holland in her colonies, England in India were all forced to take the road of expansion dictated by necessity rather than ambition, a road on which the chief difficulty is to know where to stop." For Russia, the farthest point of advance would be Chimkent. In making this declaration, Gorchakov was unaware of the fact that already, several weeks before, General Cherniaev had made a first unsuccessful attempt to capture Tashkent. This was a city far beyond the line designated in the circular as the limit of Russian penetration. The incident was typical of many. From 1865 onwards a continuous stream of 'mollifying' assurances issued from the Russian government. Each advance was the last; the most categorical instructions had been issued to prevent any forward movement. Yet each year saw another expedition and another Russian advance.

In 1865 Lord John Russell tried to negotiate an agreement defining British and Russian spheres of influence. All he was able to obtain were vague assurances of Russia's peaceful intentions. Four years later Clarendon, the British Foreign Secretary, met Gorchakov at Heidelberg and taxed him with his failure "to control the ambition of military Commanders". At the same time he proposed that Afghanistan should become a neutral buffer state. Gorchakov accepted the principle, but negotiations dragged on for several years; the two countries could not agree on the boundaries of Afghanistan. Finally, in January 1873, agreement was reached. The Russian government acknowledged that the khanate of Khiva lay outside its sphere of influence.

The agreement was not effective; Kaufmann insisted that an expedition against Khiva could no longer be deferred. In 1875 the campaign was opened. The Russian ambassador in London explained that its sole object was to rescue enslaved Russians (there were some Russian slaves in Khiva), to punish brigandage (a legitimate objective), and to teach the khan a lesson. Not only was it far from the Tsar's intentions to occupy the khanate but positive orders had been given to prevent it. The conditions imposed would be such as could not produce a prolonged occupation. By June Kaufmann was in control. The treaty imposed by him reduced the khanate to complete dependence on Russia.

The Russian treaty with Khiva formed the climax of the numerous episodes in which the professions of Gorchakov and the Tsar were belied by the men on the spot. Tashkent had been captured by Cherniaev contrary to instructions. A Chinese province had been occupied (it was later restored) against the wishes of the Foreign Ministry; the treatment of Khiva ran counter to the Tsar's formal assurances. Soon Kokand would be annexed, allegedly against his wishes. Small wonder that by the middle seventies neither the British government nor the British public attached the slightest value to Russian assurances and protestations.

Yet Alexander's unfulfilled promises were the result of weakness as much as trickery. The government at St. Petersburg had, in a large measure, lost control over its energetic agents in faraway Central Asia. Gorchakov lamented, "I am an outspoken opponent of any Russian extension whatsoever; but I can do nothing against the ambition of our generals." Miliutin was able to break Cherniaev, but could do little to assert his authority over Kaufmann and the Grand-Duke Michael. As for the Tsar himself, he was too indolent, and probably too ill-

informed, to swim against the tide of Russian imperialism. Not only were his orders ambiguous, but the men
on the spot knew only too well that they would never be
enforced. For instance, in 1875 the Tsar had vetoed
ambitious plans submitted by the Caucasian Viceroy.
He had given special instructions that nothing should
be done to inflame British susceptibilities. Yet his orders
were phrased in such a way as to sanction in advance
any step the local commanders might see fit to take.
They were "to avoid as much as possible any measures
of aggression" and "not to cross our present frontiers
without absolute necessity". Did Alexander seriously
believe that instructions such as these would restrain his
colonial soldiers? In the event, the Grand-Duke Michael
acted as though the orders did not exist. However much
the advances in Central Asia might increase Russo-
British tension, Alexander either would not or could not
control the imperialist elements in Russian society.

In a similar manner, the Tsar failed to check Pan-
Slavism, the other great expansionist force of the day.
Pan-Slavism had begun as an academic doctrine elaborated by publicists like Pogodin and Ivan Aksakov.
It had gained a foothold in the Ministries of Education and Foreign Affairs. Ignatiev, who in 1860 negotiated the Treaty of Pekin, was one of its active
exponents. Head of the influential Asiatic Department
of the Foreign Ministry since 1861, in 1864 he became
Russian Minister at Constantinople. Among the most
active Pan-Slavs was the unfortunate Empress. Ailing,
devout, and suffering in proud silence her husband's
notorious infidelity, she gave herself heart and soul to
the cause of the brother Slavs. Encouraged by her confessor, she surrounded herself with a circle of pious
elderly ladies of Pan-Slav views. The heir-apparent also
staunchly supported the 'cause'. Finally, Pan-Slavism
attracted a number of adventurers, including several
retired soldiers. Of the latter, Fadeev and Cherniaev
were perhaps the most important. Fadeev had served in

the Caucasus for twenty years under Bariatinsky, and had become an ardent supporter of Russian expansion in Central Asia. In 1867 he attacked Miliutin's reforms in a series of articles, and this ended his military career. He subsequently joined forces with Cherniaev, the conqueror of Tashkent, another soldier who had fallen foul of the powerful Minister of War. In 1869 Fadeev published a celebrated work, *Opinion on the Eastern Question*, which became, almost at once, the most widely accepted exposition of Pan-Slav doctrine.

The keynote of Fadeev's work was a violent attack on Austria-Hungary in the spirit of Paskievich's celebrated dictum that the road to Constantinople lay through Vienna. In his opinion Russia's interests in the Balkans were fundamentally opposed to those of the Dual Monarchy. It was Russia's mission to liberate the Slavs—Austria-Hungary was the chief obstacle to its accomplishment. "Austria can hold her part of the Slavonian mass as long as Turkey holds hers and vice versa." Turkey had ceased to count either as a military or a naval power. With a force of one hundred thousand men to cover the Bulgarian fortresses and a striking force of one hundred and fifty thousand, Russia could reach Constantinople within six weeks. However, the Russian lines of communication would be threatened by Austria's strategic position on the Russian flank ! (Fadeev remembered the lesson of the Crimean War; his warning was not a bad forecast of the situation which would arise in 1877.) For this reason the 'Austrian question' must be solved before it was possible to liberate the Slavs.

Here was a political programme differing profoundly from the conservative policy favoured by Alexander and Gorchakov. The Tsar disliked not only its disturbing effect on international relations but also its revolutionary implications. He was, therefore, far more wholehearted in his condemnation of Pan-Slavism than in his attempts, inspired by *raison d'état* alone, to limit the

Russian advance in Central Asia. On many occasions he criticized Pan-Slav ideas. In 1862 in his instructions to the Grand-Duke Constantine before the latter's departure for Warsaw, he uttered a warning against Pan-Slav dreams. "These ideas, however attractive they might be for the future, I consider at the present moment extremely dangerous for Russia and for the principle of monarchy. I see in their triumph a division of Russia not merely into a number of states but into separate and even hostile republics. The union of all Slavs under one head is a utopia unlikely ever to become a reality." Two years later he assured the Austrian Minister at St. Petersburg : "People fear Pan-Slavism. So far as I am concerned, I am a Russian before I am a Slav." (A recognition of realities, since hardly a drop of Slav blood flowed in Alexander's veins.) In 1867, in addressing delegates to the Moscow Slav Congress, the Tsar spoke in terms to which even the Austrian government could hardly have objected. Pan-Slavism was unacceptable to him because it spelt a (probably republican) federation including as autonomous units both Poland and the Ukraine. Moreover, as Gorchakov sensibly wrote in 1872, it was difficult to believe in "a sincere sympathy of the Slav races for *Autocratic Russia*". The Pan-Slav movement, therefore, could expect no sympathy from either the Tsar or his Minister. Yet, in the end, Alexander could control Pan-Slavism as little as 'Asiatic' expansion. A variety of circumstances drove him into the Balkan war of liberation desired by the Pan-Slavs, against the warnings of Reutern and Shuvalov, and perhaps also against his own better judgment. Once again, Alexander proved himself unable to control events.

The developments which provoked the Russo-Turkish War of 1877 began without the active participation of the Russian Pan-Slavs. In the summer of 1875 agrarian unrest developed among the Slav populations of Herzegovina (a Turkish province). Outside Slav

societies—Serbian, Austrian, Russian—began to feed
the flames. Ionin, the Russian consul-general at Ragusa
(Dubrovnik), an ardent Pan-Slav, later told a British
colleague : "I did not create the situation but I profited
from it. It began as a small stream, which might have
been lost for want of direction; so I put up a stone here
and a stone there, and kept the water together." As 1875
turned into 1876 Russian agents made their appearance
at Ragusa; the insurgents received financial support;
they were encouraged by the knowledge that they did
not stand alone.

The burning issue at this stage was the attitude of
Serbia and Montenegro, the two neighbouring Slav
principalities. In Serbia a rising tide of nationalist sentiment urged war on the side of the insurgents. Prince
Milan inquired of the Tsar whether, in the event of
intervention, Serbia could count on Russian protection
against Austria-Hungary. Alexander replied that Serbia
would have to bear alone any consequences of a possible
war with Turkey. Yet, characteristically, the Russian
answer was rather less definite than it was made to
appear. Kartsov, the consul-general in Belgrade, was a
man of little personality or ambition. A visit to St.
Petersburg showed him that Gorchakov and the Tsar
had not formulated a clear policy. He was instructed to
tell the Serbs that Russia, in conjunction with Austria-
Hungary, was working for peace. At the same time,
Russia would view without disfavour Serbian defensive
armaments if attempts to preserve peace should fail.
Returning to Belgrade, Kartsov judiciously tried to
strike a balance between these official views and the
Pan-Slav promptings of Ignatiev, his superior at Constantinople. There is little doubt that the Serbs believed
him to speak his true mind when he told them that, if
they went to war, they could in the last resort rely on
Russian support.

In May 1876 Cherniaev arrived in Belgrade. Neither
Milan nor the Serbian public could be expected to know

that he came without the blessing of the Russian government. Yet when Kartsov was summoned to Ems early in June, he found the Tsar determined on peace and angry at Cherniaev's unauthorized mission. Gorchakov, however, reminded the consul : "All the same, don't forget that, although the Tsar is against war, the heir-apparent stands at the head of the movement." Russian opinion in fact was divided; Russian diplomacy spoke with two voices. Indeed, shortly after his return to Belgrade, Kartsov received a letter from Giers, the Acting Minister of Foreign Affairs, breathing a Pan-Slav spirit and telling him not to ignore the state of Russian opinion. On June 7 Kartsov informed the Serbian government that the Tsar did not want war; within twenty-four hours he delivered a thinly disguised encouragement from Ignatiev for Serbia to go to war. Cherniaev was never disavowed. Serbia, confident of Russian support, placed her forces under his command; at the beginning of July both Serbia and Montenegro declared war on Turkey. Alexander's peace policy had been defeated by Serb impetuosity and Pan-Slav machinations. It is impossible not to feel that the Tsar had lost control of the situation.

By this time Russian opinion was in a ferment. The Bulgarian atrocities (there had been risings in Bulgaria in May cruelly suppressed by the Turks), publicized by Ignatiev and the western press, inflamed Pan-Slav indignation. Serbia's declaration of war raised excitement in St. Petersburg and Moscow to fever heat. Exaggerated reports of Serbian strength and successes appeared in the Russian press. On July 13 a special service was held by the Metropolitan of Moscow for the success of Serb and Montenegrin arms. Relief funds were set up by Slavonic Benevolent Committees. Church collections formed the largest source of funds. Khludov (who had already financed Cherniaev's mission to Belgrade) and other Moscow millionaires made impressive contributions. Whereas public collections by unofficial bodies had previously been prohibited, society ladies—including members of the Empress's entourage—began to collect money in trams, on steamboats, and in the streets. The authorities refused to intervene.

With the outbreak of fighting in the Balkans, a new field of activity opened up before the Pan-Slavs. The Red Cross, under the active patronage of the Empress, began to organize medical work on a large scale. More serious, a movement of volunteers (somewhat more genuine than some of its modern counterparts) was started. A recruiting office was opened without interference from the authorities. The chief of staff of the Corps of Guards, an ardent Pan-Slav and confidant of the Tsarevich, encouraged Guards officers to volunteer for service in Serbia. They had to resign their commissions, but were promised reinstatement. The departure of volunteer trains (vividly described at the end of Tolstoy's *Anna Karenina*) was accompanied by patriotic manifestations fully reported in the Russian press. The actual number of volunteers is estimated at 4,000 to 5,000, including some eight hundred officers. Some of the latter were regulars and highly placed in society. The movement had developed without the sanction of the Tsar and his Ministers, a fact almost unheard of in the annals of Russian history. Ivan Aksakov, looking back on the Pan-Slav campaign, wrote: "Public opinion conducted a war apart from the government and without any state organization, in a foreign state." It was a challenge to the authority of the Tsar and his advisers.

Alexander and Gorchakov returned to Russia from Germany in the middle of July, when the Pan-Slav campaign was in full swing. Katkov, in alliance with the Moscow merchants and the cotton millionaire Tretiakov, was appealing for funds for the Serbs and Bulgars. Cherniaev and his doings were exploited; when his personal failings and military defeats could no longer be concealed, Katkov demanded that the European powers should save the Serbs. This, however, did not prevent him from publishing violent attacks on England and later on Austria. In the face of these vociferous activities, the Tsar and his Ministers tried —ineffectually—to assert their authority. In August Alexander assured Reutern of his determination not to go to war. Early in September the first half-hearted steps were taken to curtail the activities of the "Slavonic Benevolent Committees". Cherniaev's proclamation of Serbian independence was followed by a prohibition of 'volunteering' from the active army. Gorchakov attempted to check Katkov's hysterical anti-British campaign. None of these measures proved very effective. Restrictions imposed on the "Slavonic Benevolent Committees" were soon withdrawn, it was believed, at the instance of the Empress. In October the press, led by Katkov, resumed its attacks—this time against Austria.

During the autumn foreign observers began to express doubts whether the Tsar would be able to resist Pan-Slav pressure. The 'activist' forces were impressive: the Orthodox Church linked in unnatural alliance with the Old Believer millionaires of Moscow; the Empress and her coterie; the Tsarevich with all those who looked to the coming reign; soldiers and sailors who swam with the tide, whether from conviction or interest; last, but not least, the press, led by the indefatigable Katkov and the able propagandist Aksakov. Against this formidable array stood a handful of pacific Ministers (Reutern, Valuiev, Miliutin, and Timashev, the Minister of the Interior, occasionally supported by the senile Gorchakov) and the German element among the soldiers and bureaucrats. Yet the Pan-Slav Movement, however impressive in appearance, was a movement of 'public opinion' rather than of the masses. Few of the volunteers came from the ranks of the peasantry. In September the abject failure of Cherniaev and the Serbs produced second thoughts even amongst the upper classes.

The star of Pan-Slavism was waning. The Tsar was free to determine Russian policy almost independently of Pan-Slav effervescence.

At Livadia in the Crimea in the autumn, Alexander conferred with his closest advisers. Adlerberg and Gorchakov, Miliutin and Reutern with their assistants, were in attendance. Ignatiev came from Constantinople. The Tsarevich was summoned to attend. The Grand-Duke Nicholas, the Tsar's soldier brother, was called in. The Empress was present, attended by her ladies and by a chaplain in close touch with the Moscow "Slavonic Benevolent Committee". The question of war or peace was debated. Reutern submitted a secret memorandum explaining that war would ruin his financial reforms. Miliutin and Totleben, the hero of Sevastopol, were lukewarm. The majority of those present recommended a 'national' policy from which at least the possibility of war was not excluded. The Tsar, influenced by "a feminine atmosphere of exalted nationalism", agreed to partial mobilization. A plan of campaign was approved; the Grand-Dukes Nicholas and Michael were appointed commanders-in-chief respectively of the Danubian and Caucasian armies. If this was not yet a decision for war, it was a long step towards it.

In fact, Alexander still hoped to secure 'peace with honour', by which he understood far-reaching concessions to the Balkan Christians. If this proved impossible to attain, Russia would go to war. Such was the programme announced to the Russian public in the celebrated Moscow speech of November 11. "I know", Alexander told an enthusiastic gathering, "that all Russia shares with me the deepest interest in the sufferings of our brothers in faith and origin; but for me the true interests of Russia are dearer than everything else, and I would do my utmost to avoid the shedding of precious Russian blood. That is why I have tried and am still trying to bring about by peaceful means a real improvement in the life of all the Christian inhabitants of the Balkan peninsula. Discussions among representatives of the six great powers will shortly open at Constantinople to arrange conditions of peace. I sincerely desire agreement. If, however, there is no agreement, if I see that we cannot obtain such guarantees as will ensure the satisfaction of our just demands . . . then I am determined to act independently. I am convinced that in such an eventuality all Russia will respond to my appeal ... May God help us to fulfil our sacred mission." Two days later the Tsar ordered the mobilization of six army corps and the corresponding reserves.

The Russian government was now committed to a policy which must result either in substantial guarantees for the Balkan Christians or in military intervention. For several months the Tsar continued to work for a pacific solution. The six powers agreed on a settlement, setting up autonomous states in eastern and western Bulgaria. The Porte rejected the proposals. Thereupon, Alexander, in a manifesto of April 24 (1877), informed his subjects that Russia was at war with Turkey.

How far was Pan-Slav agitation responsible for driving Russia into war? It is certain that the Pan-Slavs played an active part in the early stages of the crisis, first by keeping alive the rising in Herzegovina and later in encouraging Serbian intervention. In this phase, Pan-Slav activities ran counter to official policy, and Alexander and Gorchakov were faced with a *fait accompli*. On the other hand, it would be wrong to say that the Russian government itself was driven into war. The Pan-Slav Movement in Russia reached its peak during August and September (1876), after which enthusiasm began to wane. Moreover, the decisions of Livadia—reminiscent of similar decisions taken by Nicholas I on the eve of the Crimean War—were taken at a spot far removed from noisy Pan-Slav pressure. If Alexander was subjected to moral pressure it was mainly from members of his own family. The evidence suggests that, even after partial mobilization, he still

155

hoped for a peaceful outcome. The decision to go to war was in the end taken in cool deliberation by the Tsar and his official advisers.

The war, tardily but not unwillingly begun, brought the Russians a series of disappointments. The Grand-Duke Nicholas proved himself an incompetent commander. The hospital and commissariat services, in spite of Miliutin's reforms, proved scarcely more satisfactory than they had been in the Crimean War. The Turks' heroic defence of Plevna held up the Russian advance for several crucial months. During this delay, Anglo-Austrian hostility began to crystallize. When the Russians finally reached the outskirts of Constantinople and Ignatiev imposed on the defeated Turks the Treaty of San Stefano, it was already too late : a British squadron was securely anchored in the Bosphorus. England and Austria appeared ready to declare war; nothing beyond a benevolent neutrality was to be obtained from Bismarck. Faced with the danger of a powerful coalition, the Russian government surrendered to the pressure of Europe. During tense weeks of negotiation, agreement was reached to 'revise' Ignatiev's treaty. The main change, agreed to at the Congress of Berlin, was that Russia should give up her big Bulgarian state. The other major decision was that Bosnia and Herzegovina were to pass under Austrian control. This settlement—although accompanied by considerable Russian gains (in Asia Minor and Bessarabia) and the creation of a small Bulgarian state—caused bitter disappointment in Russia. A general feeling of disillusionment succeeded the Pan-Slav fervour of 1876 and the patriotic enthusiasm of the war. The settlement of 1878 was considered—unjustly—a Russian defeat like that of 1856. The net result of Pan-Slav dreams was an apathy and irritation dangerous to the Tsar.

Alexander's attitude towards expansionist forces in Russian society had been, from the start, ambiguous.

Too cautious to approve unreservedly the dangerous schemes of a Kaufmann or an Ignatiev, he at no time took effective steps to curb their expansionist ardour. Apart from a few officers removed for their opposition to Miliutin, not a single one of the empire builders or Pan-Slav enthusiasts was ever dismissed from his post or even reprimanded. As a moderate imperialist, Alexander welcomed any development conducive to the power and greatness of Russia. Desiring the ends without the means and torn by conflicting sentiments, his orders lacked vigour and firmness. In consequence, they were disregarded—usually with impunity—alike by empire builders and Pan-Slav publicists. Resolute agents of expansion would adopt the policy of the *fait accompli*—knowing in the event of success that their actions would be condoned and even praised. Yet it is difficult to blame Alexander too severely for his weakness. While trying half-heartedly to curb the more flagrant acts of men who, after all, remained his loyal subjects, he was engaged in a deadly struggle with forces of subversion which threatened to undermine his authority and the security of the state.

## Chapter Eight

# The Tsar Martyr

FOR some years after the establishment of police rule in 1866, the revolutionary movement in Russia was at a low ebb. By 1869 there were signs of a revival. Groups of revolutionaries were coming into being in many parts of the empire. The most important of these, composed mainly of young intellectuals of the upper and middle classes, students and army officers, had agents in some thirty provinces. Their ranks were swelled by students expelled from the universities after the disorders of 1869. Then in 1873 the Russian government had the unwisdom to order all Russians studying at foreign universities (especially Geneva) to return. By this decision further reinforcements were provided for the revolutionary groups.

During the late sixties and early seventies revolutionary leaders had given out the slogan 'to the people', to increase contacts of the revolutionaries with workers and peasants. In consequence, in the summer of 1874, thousands of young men and women invaded the countryside, clad as peasants, in an attempt to convert the villagers to socialism. Their efforts met with little success : the peasants proved apathetic and even hostile. Shuvalov's police were active in breaking up the movement. Some 800 agitators had been seized by the end of the summer. After prolonged investigations two groups of 193 and 50 were held for trial.

Undeterred by their first failure, the revolutionaries still at large attempted a second 'going to the people' in 1876. This time, to gain the respect of the peasants, they went as petty officials, teachers, artisans, and shop-keepers. The peasants again remained almost wholly indifferent, and the movement, like its predecessors, exhausted itself without effect. The revolutionaries then decided to create a more effective organization. 'Land and Liberty' was directed by a 'basic group', divided into a number of sections. The 'administrative section' located in St. Petersburg issued general political directives and was responsible for the issue of false passports. There were three separate sections for propaganda among the intelligentsia, the factory workers, and the peasants. The 'disorganizing section' was responsible for the rescue of arrested comrades from prison, the protection of 'revolutionary honour' (which meant the assassination of traitors and police spies), and the protection of members against the police. 'Land and Liberty' owned a secret press bought abroad but operated in St. Petersburg. Provincial groups were autonomous in the conduct of their own affairs but responsible to the 'basic group' for their activities. The 'basic group', whenever necessary, would summon a meeting of the 'council', composed of all members present in St. Petersburg at the time. Such was the body which now began to pit its forces against the Tsar and his government.

In December 1876, on the eve of the Turkish War, a small revolutionary demonstration was organized in a snowstorm outside the Kazan Cathedral in St. Petersburg. It was easily dispersed and many arrests were made. In February and March 1877 the government staged the first mass trial of revolutionaries. Another major trial, that 'of the 193', opened in the autumn. As the accused were tried by the new courts, sentences were comparatively lenient. Of the 193 accused, no fewer than 153 were acquitted. Many of those found guilty received only light sentences. The Tsar was displeased and increased many sentences; a number of those acquitted by the courts were sent into exile away in the interior. The trial of the 193 was followed by a *cause célèbre* which marked the beginning of open war between the revolutionaries and the government.

Among those arrested after the demonstration outside the Kazan Cathedral was Bogoliubov, an ex-student and 'veteran' revolutionary. One day in prison he refused to salute Trepov during an inspection. The all-powerful police chief thereupon ordered Bogoliubov to be flogged for insubordination. The flogging provoked a demonstration among the other prisoners; several revolutionary groups prepared to punish Trepov. They were anticipated by a woman revolutionary, the famous Vera Zasulich, who on her own initiative fired at and severely wounded him in January 1878. She made no attempt to escape and stood her trial in April. Amid tremendous excitement the jury, after brief deliberation, returned a verdict of 'not guilty'. There was enthusiastic applause from the packed galleries, those demonstrating their approval including generals and high officials. There was a tumult outside the court building when the police tried to rearrest her. She was spirited away by her friends, and after hiding for some time in the capital was able to escape to Switzerland. The government, in impotent fury, decreed that in future all matters of 'resistance to the authorities, rebellion, assassination or attempts on the lives of officials' would be tried by military courts. It was a declaration of war against the revolutionaries.

The growing ferment was not confined to the capital. At Odessa some days after Zasulich's attempt on Trepov, Kovalski, a prominent revolutionary, defended himself with revolver and dagger when trying to resist arrest. At Kiev an unsuccessful attempt on the life of the assistant prosecutor was followed by the armed efforts of two revolutionaries to resist arrest. Leaflets were distributed, signed by 'the Executive Committee of the Russian Social Revolutionary Party'. The students of Kiev demonstrated. Large numbers were excluded from the university and fifteen banished from the city.

Their passage through Moscow provoked demonstrations and scuffles. A police officer in Kiev was fatally injured.

Unrest at Kiev and Odessa was followed by a daring stroke in the capital itself. In broad daylight, in one of the city's busiest thoroughfares, Kravchinski (alias Stepniak), a former artillery officer, cut down Mezentsev, the head of the Third Division, with a sword. Kravchinski managed to escape and lived to publish his memoirs in London. 'Land and Liberty' distributed a leaflet entitled 'A Death for a Death', justifying the murder. (During the summer, political prisoners in the fortress of SS. Peter and Paul had organized a hunger strike, when several had died. Kravchinski's action was justified as a reprisal.)

Other acts of violence followed. Early in 1879 a revolutionary killed Prince Kropotkin (a cousin of Peter Kropotkin, the anarchist), the Governor-General of Charkov, where student riots had been suppressed with severity. As usual, the assassin was able to make good his escape. A subsequent attempt on Drenteln, the new head of the Third Division, was unsuccessful. The climax of the campaign came in April, when Soloviev (without the official consent of 'Land and Liberty') fired on the Tsar himself outside the Winter Palace. Five shots missed Alexander, who escaped unhurt, Soloviev paid the penalty of his crime.

The most alarming feature for the government, however, were not the acts of revolutionary violence—striking though they were—but the attitude of the Russian public. The acquittal of Vera Zasulich had been a 'slap in the face' for the government, and the applause of the public had underlined the fact. Again, had the public felt the slightest sympathy for the authorities, Kravchinski could never have escaped after killing Mezentsev in broad daylight in the centre of St. Petersburg. The escape of other revolutionary terrorists was made possible only by the complete apathy of the public. When the government turned to the zemstvos for support, it received the reply that, until the Russian public received greater freedom to express its views, it could take no part in the struggle. Indeed, certain zemstvo leaders were engaged in abortive negotiations with 'Land and Liberty' about joint action in favour of constitutional government. Revelations of corruption in the supply services of the Russian armies and the diplomatic defeat at the Congress of Berlin increased the hostility of wider sections of the Russian public. There was widespread opposition to the police system of Shuvalov's incompetent successors. The mood of the Russian public favoured the activities of the revolutionaries.

Even within the charmed circle of Court and official society the Tsar had by this time become very unpopular. His relations with Catherine Dolgoruky were public property. To help the police protect his life, his second family was now moved to the Winter Palace itself. There the Empress Mary was approaching the term of her unhappy life. As she lay dying she could hear playing in the room above her her husband's children by his 'second wife'. By this time conservative circles in the two capitals, led by the Tsarevich, hardly forbore even in public from showing their detestation of Catherine and her children. The Grand-Duchesses in particular repulsed any attempt of the Tsar to introduce the princess into the domestic circle. The unhappy Emperor was surrounded by tension and strife even in his intimate private life. A palace revolution seemed not at all impossible.

Alexander now lived in semi-isolation, surrounded by a small group of personal friends, of whom the amiable gambler Sasha Adlerberg was the most conspicuous. To these were added some 'liberal' politicians like Abaza and Valuiev, protégés of the princess. Finally, some faithful but insignificant officials loyally stood by their master. The Tsar was isolated from the Russian people, unpopular with the educated public, and cut off from the bulk of society and the Court. His fate had become a matter of indifference to the majority of his subjects.

This situation was bound to have its effects on a personality as impressionable as the Tsar's. In the summer of 1878 he returned to his capital, after a prolonged absence, looking exhausted and suffering from a nervous collapse which he tried to conceal. He was drained of energy at a moment when he needed it more than ever. The Empress continued to play her difficult role with dignity, but she had aged even more rapidly than her husband. Receptions were held as before, but the atmosphere had changed. Everywhere in the vicinity of the Court police precautions were in evidence. On ceremonial drives the Tsar was accompanied by an escort of Cossacks. "One feels", noted an observer, "that the ground is shaking and the building threatened with collapse; the inhabitants behave as if they did not notice the fact; the masters perceive darkly the coming disaster but conceal their innermost fears."

Alexander himself had become cynical and disillusioned. When told that someone had spoken ill of him, he observed : "Strange, I don't remember ever having done him a favour; why then should he hate me?" When asked if that was really his opinion of people, he replied : "Yes, that is what I have learnt in the bitter school of experience; all I have to do to make an enemy is to do someone a favour." Sunk in bitterness and disillusionment, Alexander now felt more than ever the need for affection which he could hope to find only in the bosom of his second family. His love for Catherine and her children increased with every day; to provide for their future, to give them a legitimate status in the eyes of the world, to make the woman who had sacrificed everything for him Empress, became the object of his every thought. Compared to this, matters of state were of secondary importance. In this frame of mind,

Alexander was ill-fitted to lead the forces of authority in their life-and-death struggle with revolutionary terrorists.

Soloviev's attempt was followed by renewed efforts to stamp out the revolutionary movement. Governors-General with emergency powers were appointed for the whole of Russia. Under their direction military courts began to operate; within a few months some dozen revolutionaries had ended their lives on the gallows. Gurko, the new Governor-General of St. Petersburg, went about his business with calm determination. He expressed the well-founded conviction that the number of active revolutionaries was small. The new measures appeared to produce results. During the summer of 1879, acts of revolutionary violence ceased. Superficially, the streets of the capital resumed their normal appearance. It was the calm before the storm.

'Land and Liberty', in fact, was passing through a crisis. Soloviev's attempt had been made without orders from the organization. Its members were profoundly divided between those advocating terrorist methods (the followers of Bakunin) and those who preferred the earlier policy of peaceful propaganda. Among the chief advocates of terror were Mikhailov, the leader of the movement, and Zheliabov from Odessa. In the summer of 1879 the old 'Land and Liberty' was dissolved and replaced by two daughter organizations; the 'Black Partition', which favoured peaceful methods, and the terrorist 'People's Will'. The latter group was led by the formidable Mikhailov. He was the security expert of the terrorists. An adept at secret correspondence and the manufacture of false documents, he had thoroughly familiarized himself with the geography of St. Petersburg. He knew most of the connecting passages and houses with more than one entrance, and was an expert at shaking off police agents. He succeeded in introducing one of his followers, Kletochnikov, into the headquarters of the Third Division. In this way he learnt of the existence of a police spy in his own organization, who was promptly 'liquidated'. On September 7, 1879, the Central Executive Committee of the 'People's Will' formally condemned Alexander Romanov to death. From now on every effort of the movement was directed to his assassination.

The first attempt was to be made on the train in which the Tsar returned from a visit to the Crimea. Preparations were made in three places to blow up the train. Alexander did not pass the first (in Odessa). At the second the mine failed to explode. But on December 1 a train was overturned by an explosion a few miles outside Moscow. However, it was not the train in which the Tsar was travelling, but only a baggage train sent in advance of the imperial party. If the Tsar escaped with his life, so did the terrorists in each of the three attempts. Three days after the Moscow explosion, the paper of the 'People's Will' published an appeal to the Tsar. The organization, it declared, had vowed merciless war against him as the embodiment of reaction and repression. However, he would be 'pardoned' if he agreed to call a Constituent Assembly. It is hardly surprising that the offer met with no response.

The authorities were perplexed and the Third Division was powerless. A German historian who has examined its records remarks on "the incredible powerlessness and incompetence of the institution". In 1878 Alexander called for the names of ringleaders of the revolutionary movement : the Third Division could name only one. For the rest the Tsar was informed that the number of the revolutionaries seemed to have unaccountably grown. It would continue to do so until the leaders were destroyed. Another report described the situation as serious but not hopeless. Final victory was guaranteed by the boundless affection of the entire people, the army, and the landowning nobility for His Majesty's sacred person. Later, the head of the Division reported 'with sad and heavy feelings' the appearance of the first issue of 'The People's Will'. Forty-three searches had failed to reveal a single copy of the paper. At last several copies were discovered in the pockets of a careless Jewish revolutionary in the public library at St. Petersburg. After an investigation lasting eighteen months the secret terrorist press remained undiscovered. The revolutionaries were aided by Kletochnikov, who repeatedly gave warning of impending police raids. When the Tsar taxed the head of the Third Division with his lack of success, he received the reply that the revolutionary party was vigilantly watched. To soften the reproach Alexander observed amiably that his criticism applied to all branches of the administration 'since we are inclined to go to sleep'.

But the revolutionaries were not 'inclined to go to sleep'. With feverish energy they were preparing a new attempt. Khalturin, one of the founders of the Moscow Workers' Union, was a skilful carpenter with numerous acquaintances among the St. Petersburg workers. In the autumn of 1879, thanks to several high recommendations, he secured employment in the Winter Palace. In the disorganization during the Emperor's absence, he managed to introduce a quantity of explosives into the Palace. These he stored under his pillow in a basement room. The German government warned the Russian government that an attempt was impending. It drew attention to the basement as a danger spot. A revolutionary arrested by the Russian police was found carrying a sketch of the Palace, with a spot in the basement marked with a red cross. The special police in the Palace were reinforced; surprise checks were carried out day and night. Again everything was inefficient and nothing was discovered.

On the evening of February 17, 1880, a violent explosion shook the Winter Palace. The dining-room, where the imperial family were about to entertain the Prince of Bulgaria, was only slightly damaged. In the room below some forty Finnish soldiers of the guard lay in their blood. Khalturin got away to continue his revolutionary activities in southern Russia. The reaction of the upper classes to the attempt was one of utter indifference. Schweinitz, the German ambassador, has described the fatal evening. The fashionable world of the capital was gathering for dinner at the residence of the French ambassador. As the guests were assembling, Giers (the effective head of the Foreign Ministry) told Schweinitz that, on entering his coach, he had heard an explosion from the direction of the Palace. He had sent a servant to inquire. Schweinitz was horrified at the conduct of Giers, the Tsar's 'best and most honourable' Minister, who had calmly driven past the Palace to his dinner after hearing a violent explosion. When the servant arrived with the news of what had occurred, Schweinitz left the dinner in disgust—not before having given 'a piece of his mind' to a general of the imperial suite who was calmly sipping his coffee by the fireside. When, a few hours later, the ambassador presented himself at the Palace, he found the Tsar enjoying his usual game of whist. "God has saved me again", he said, embracing Schweinitz. The Empress, who knew nothing of the attempt, had slept quietly all night. The public was apathetic: there was not the slightest movement in the streets. The middle classes were completely indifferent, while society was pursuing its pleasures. "One is tempted", Schweinitz observed, "to regard as moribund a social body which fails to react to such a shock."

The apathy of the Russian public in the face of repeated terrorist attempts led the more intelligent and responsible of the Tsar's Ministers to seek a way of conciliating public opinion. Both Valuiev and the Grand-Duke Constantine brought forward again proposals for advisory constitutional bodies which they had first suggested in the sixties. After some hesitation, Alexander agreed that the subject should be discussed, and, early in 1880, held several meetings in private with his confidential advisers. Valuiev's and Constantine's proposals were rejected. The Tsarevich bitterly attacked their 'liberalism' and demanded that all government departments should be placed under one central directing authority. He recommended a Supreme Commission, similar to the commissions of inquiry set up in 1862 and 1866 but with vastly extended powers. The Tsar accepted the idea. At the head of the new Commission he placed an Armenian, General Loris-Melikov, who since 1879 had been Governor-General of Charkov. In this office he had succeeded in combining sternness in the struggle against revolution with consideration for the population at large. These appeared to be qualities desirable in the new 'dictator'.

The powers now granted to Loris were almost 'autocratic'. The Commission was to exercise supreme power in the empire: all civil and military authorities had to carry out its orders. Loris himself had chosen his own colleagues on this all-powerful body. His 'cabinet' included Pobedonostsev, ideologist of reaction and confidant of the Tsarevich, two generals, and a number of senators and high officials. Moreover Loris, like Shuvalov before him, had accepted office on his own terms. He wrung from the reluctant Tsar permission to unite the different police administrations. The Third Division lost its autonomy and was absorbed into a general police department headed by Plehve, a conservative official. Loris also secured the dismissal of the obscurantist Tolstoy and his replacement as Minister of Education by a liberal, Saburov. The incompetent Minister of Finance (the successor of Reutern, who had resigned in protest against the Turkish war) made way for the liberal Abaza. There were other changes of lesser importance in the personnel of the government. For the second time in his reign Alexander had abdicated his powers, this time into the hands of an 'unnatural' coalition between conservative critics (the Tsarevich, Pobedonostsev, Plehve) and 'liberals' grouped around Catherine Dolgoruky (Loris and Abaza). Thus began what critics soon came to describe as the 'Dictatorship of the Heart'.

The policy of the new government was essentially one of relaxation and concession to moderate opinion. Once again, as at the beginning of the reign, prisoners were released. The press was given greater freedom. Abaza's first act was the removal of the oppressive tax on salt. The basis of Loris's programme was the belated application, in the spirit as well as the letter, of the great zemstvo and judicial reforms. Restrictions imposed on the zemstvos were eased, so that even the radical zemstvo of Tver expressed satisfaction at the dictator's efforts to improve relations between government and public. Such repression as there was became unobtrusive : only a few revolutionary leaders were quietly arrested. Early in May the German ambassador noted that ten weeks of the new administration had produced a general relaxation of tension, however ephemeral it might prove to be.

A new crisis, however, was approaching, provoked by the Tsar's irresponsible infatuation. In June 1880 the Empress died, and forty days later (the minimum prescribed by the Orthodox Church), Alexander married—morganatically—the lady who for many years had been his wife in all but name. In December she was raised to the rank of Princes Yurievskaya (the family name of the Romanovs). Early in the new year, in the company of eight-year-old 'Gogo' (her oldest son, Prince George), she began to share the meals of the imperial family. During these meals the Tsar (now sixty-three years of age) behaved like a lover of eighteen. When he invited those around him to share in his happiness, the response of the imperial family was icy. The Grand-Duchesses detested the princess as an upstart, but her bitterest enemy was the Tsarevich. It had been anticipated that, when the Empress died, Alexander would not only marry Catherine but secure her coronation. (Catherine considered that, as a descendant of St. Vladimir, she was entitled to this honour.) An impassioned protest against any such proceeding was registered by Alexander Alexandrovich; there were reports of violent altercations between father and son.

While Alexander was storing up new troubles for himself, Loris had successfully— or so he thought— completed his policy of pacification. Six months after its creation, the Supreme Executive Commission was dissolved. Loris now assumed the functions of Minister of the Interior. His position resembled that of a prime minister or, as Valuiev jokingly called it, a 'First Boyar'. At a 'press conference' in September 1880, Loris asked editors not to excite the public with speculations about constitutional changes. Some months later he asked provincial Governors to encourage the zemstvos to discuss the state of the peasantry. He also ordered senatorial inspections in various provinces, and let it be known that the results would be examined by the government in conjunction with representatives of the public. Loris submitted to the Emperor that it was his policy to satisfy the loyal elements among the liberals. To do this, he proposed the formation of two Commissions to prepare legislation: one to deal with administrative and economic, the other with financial matters. The Commissions would be composed of officials, zemstvo representatives, professors, and publicists. Their drafts would come before a General Commission, to be composed of the two Preparatory Commissions together with two elected 'experts' from each provincial zemstvo and major city.

The inspiration of the proposal, which might have paved the way for a peaceful transition from autocracy to a semi-constitutional monarchy, came not from Loris but from Abaza. The Minister of Finance worked on the Tsar through Princess Yurievskaya by representing to her—possibly with some justice—that a concession of this kind would reconcile some of the public to the proposed coronation. The two events might well be announced in the same manifesto. Alexander was willing to pay this price to obtain public acquiescence in the achievement of his dearest wish. At a special meeting of advisers under Valuiev's presidency even the Tsarevich did not veto the Abaza proposals.

While these 'constitutional' plans were being matured, the government had been winning its long-drawn-out battle with the terrorists. Misled by the police about the extent of their knowledge, a captured terrorist had inadvertently given detailed information about their organization. As a result of the numerous arrests and deportations which followed, the terrorist organization shrunk to a mere handful. The surviving leaders felt that the sands were running out. A last grand attempt was planned. For months a detailed study had been made of the Emperor's movements. One of the principal arteries of St. Petersburg was mined, and a shaft driven under a lesser street used by the Emperor. It had been filled with enough explosives to blow the near-by buildings sky-high. To make doubly sure, four young terrorists volunteered to throw bombs at the Emperor. The plans were in an advanced stage when, on March 11, 1881, Zheliabov, the leader of the organization, was arrested. The arrest of the remainder might now be a matter of hours. The terrorists, led by a woman, Sophia Perovskaya, resolved at the earliest opportunity to carry out their attempt.

Loris also knew that the situation was becoming critical. "There need only be another unfortunate shot", he had told a high official, "and I am lost and with me my entire system." On 12 March Loris reported to the Emperor the results of Zheliabov's first interrogation. The prisoner had refused to give any information and boasted that his arrest would not prevent another attempt. Loris warned the Tsar, in the presence of the Tsarevich, not to attend the usual Sunday parade the following day. If he insisted on doing so, special precautions must be taken. In fact, all that was humanly possible had already been done in the streets he was likely to pass. For the last three weeks, Princess Yurievskaya had dissuaded her husband from attending the Sunday parades. Now, seeing him completely calm after his talk with Loris, she made no effort to do so again. A visit to the ailing Loris at his home confirmed her in a sense of security. That night, taking her arm to lead her to dinner, Alexander remarked: "I am so happy at present that this happiness frightens me." He spent the evening—as on several previous occasions—telling his son George what to do if he suddenly lost his father.

Alexander had taken a decision. On Sunday, March 13, he received Loris to give his personal approval to the constitutional changes now recommended. Having signed the document, the Tsar went to inspect the parade. His wife had specially asked him to avoid two streets—which happened to be the streets mined by the conspirators. After the parade, he paid a call on his cousin, the Grand-Duchess Catherine. He imparted to her his decision to sanction the participation of elected members in his legislative commissions, and took his leave.

It had long been the practice for the Emperor to return to the Palace by a different route from that by which he had come. The return route he would announce only at the last moment. This time his return drive took him through Catherine Street along a canal of the same name. As the sledge entered this quiet street —which, contrary to the assurances of the Minister of Police, had not been closed to the public—a mining student, Ryssakov, threw a bomb. Alexander was unhurt. Against the advice of his driver, he stepped out of the sledge to look after the wounded cossacks of the escort. "Thank God, no", he replied to a question from bystanders if he was wounded. "Thank God?" exclaimed at that moment another terrorist (Hriniewicki, a Polish student at the Technological Institute), and hurled a bomb directly at the Emperor's feet. Both the

Tsar's legs were shattered. To his brother Michael, who arrived upon the scene, he could only whisper : "Home to the Palace, to die there." In Michael's arms the dying Emperor was taken by sledge to the Winter Palace, escorted by bleeding cossacks on bespattered horses. The Princess Yurievskaya was waiting for her husband, expecting to accompany him on a stroll through the Summer Garden.

Any emotion felt in Russia at the news of the assassination was neither widespread nor sincere. The popular attitude at St. Petersburg was a blend of indifference and curiosity. No indignation was felt against the terrorists, there were no lamentations or expressions of grief. For a little while a few hundred people gathered each day at the place of the attempt; some wept and brought flowers and wreaths. The funeral cortège from the Palace to the fortress was hasty and disorderly; the conventions of common decency were barely maintained. The populace remained stubbornly unmoved. The feeling of the upper classes was, perhaps, best expressed by the honest Schweinitz. Asked why he did not show more grief at the death of a sovereign to whom he had been sincerely devoted (Schweinitz and Alexander had been inseparable hunting companions), the German ambassador replied : "We have already grieved for him" ("*nous en avons fait notre deuil*"). "After the war and through his fatal relationship with the woman he loved, he was too greatly changed. God has saved him from losing still more of his dignity and self-respect. His death we should regard as a blessing, if only the circumstances had been less cruel."

The circumstances of Alexander's death underline his tragic personal failure. Except at brief moments during the liberation struggle, and later during the Polish insurrection, he had never been a popular ruler. His personality—however charming in an intimate circle, and particularly in the company of children—was reserved and haughty. The pleasantness and suavity of his manner was broken all too easily by out-bursts of temper. Both the Tsar's private life and that of his entourage brought the dynasty reproach. Nor did Alexander possess many of the qualities indispensable to a successful ruler. From his childhood he had tried to evade difficulties, to find an easy escape from complex situations. What had been a venial sin in the pupil of Merder and Zhukovsky, became a serious fault in the autocratic Emperor of All the Russias. A sense of duty instilled by his father had prevented the Tsar from becoming *Alexandre le Bien Aimé*—another Louis XV—but the tenacity and concern for the public welfare shown in the struggle for liberation later evaporated. A sense of insecurity and apprehension made Alexander the 'prisoner' first of Shuvalov and Trepov, later of Loris-Melikov. His ill-starred infatuation for Catherine Dolgoruky became a scandal to the state which undermined his own authority and destroyed the respect of his subjects.

Alexander's personal failings aggravated his already difficult task of reconciling the increase of freedom with the preservation of imperial authority. Peter the Great, Nicholas I, and Lenin did not experience this conflict: they were autocrats who knew not the meaning of liberty. Alexander, on the other hand, although not a liberal himself, was born into an age when liberalism was in the ascendant. The teachings of Zhukovsky, reaction against the régime of Nicholas, popular expectations and demands, combined with the impetuosity of the Grand-Duke Constantine, carried him into concessions to the liberal *Zeitgeist* against his inclination. These concessions, half-hearted though they were, produced the general ferment of opinion inseparable from a Russian 'thaw'. Alexander's 'mildness' led to a general loosening of the reins of government. The Russian public, unprepared for freedom, indulged in extravagant criticism which threatened to undermine the authority of the Tsar and his government. By 1861, with student and peasant unrest, subversion in the army, incipient rebellion in Poland, and incendiarism in the capital, it appeared that Russia was slipping into chaos; liberty was degenerating into licence.

Yet Alexander was a pupil of Nicholas much more than a pupil of Zhukovsky. He was at heart a believer in order, authority, and autocracy. In his view everything at home must come from above and be carefully controlled and supervised; abroad, there must be order, authority, and a respect for existing rights and obligations. With a disposition in itself autocratic, Alexander naturally turned to reaction—some would say the defence of his legitimate authority—when subversive movements made their appearance.

It was, however, precisely as an autocrat that Alexander was the greatest failure. Throughout his reign order was not effectively maintained, authority never secure. Characteristically, he flouted the wishes of his parents by his marriage to the Princess Mary. Again, in his private and family life he failed to set an example of order. Leading an irregular life himself he was unable to rebuke others—in this way very much unlike his father. The absence of a firm paternal or fraternal authority in the imperial family became notorious. Nor could the Emperor's entourage—from the gambler Sasha Adlerberg to Catherine's stock-jobbing friends—inspire much respect. The Tsarevich consistently opposed Alexander in his later years, and did not scruple to criticize his father's private and public conduct. The Tsar was never master in his own house. A court rent by factions and intrigues can be no secure basis of authority for an absolute government in troubled times.

The disorder spread outwards from the centre. There was no unity in the government. Ministers of divergent views fought and intrigued against each other; important political decisions were made according to the constellation of the moment. The Emperor, it was said, gave his voice to whoever had spoken to him last. Alexander had no Richelieu or Bismarck, but only a Gorchakov. Shuvalov, his ablest Minister, fell victim to an intrigue engineered by the Princess Catherine. Loris's power was based on a precarious coalition brought about by an emergency. If there was no cohesion in the government in distant St. Petersburg, there could be no order among its local agents scattered over the vast empire. Alexander could exercise effective control neither over the powerful proconsuls in Tiflis and Tashkent, nor yet over Katkov, the eloquent demagogue, ambitious liars like Ignatiev, or even a windy adventurer like Cherniaev. Acts of defiance and insubordination enough to cause Nicholas I to turn in his grave were committed with impunity every day.

Alexander proved himself not only a disappointing 'liberal'—if indeed that term can be applied to him—but, more seriously, an inefficient autocrat. While he would not give his educated subjects the constitution for which they clamoured, he failed to use to advantage the autocratic powers which he felt impelled to retain. He merely succeeded in proving that a pseudo-liberal autocrat is an unhappy hybrid unlikely to achieve political success. The narrow principles of Nicholas I or Alexander III, for whom Alexander's problems did not exist, proved—on a short-term view—more effective than the unsuccessful attempt to combine authority and freedom.

Yet Alexander's policy of combining reform with control from above was not, in itself, unsound. He was right in initiating long-overdue reforms; one cannot blame him for trying to carry them into effect through the existing machinery of government. Such a policy, however, was likely to be opposed from two different directions. Reform could not but hurt the vested interests of landowners, merchants, and officials; refusal to admit the participation of the public in government could not but antagonize the liberals. Alexander's reign combined reform and repression; the combination pleased no important section of the population. Conservatives would have preferred less reform and more control; the liberals the opposite. Alexander, working for the public welfare according to his lights, succeeded in antagonizing both groups at the same time. A gulf began to open between the Russian government and the public never again to be closed. Loris's administration—so nearly successful yet, in the event, so tragically abortive—was the last attempt of tsarism to come to terms with liberal Russian opinion. Could Loris have succeeded in his policy of organic institutional development? Could even he have successfully counteracted the effects of the Tsar's unpopular liaison and Catherine's probable coronation? It seems more than likely that, had Alexander once again escaped the assassin, he would have fallen to a peaceful palace 'revolution' and abdicated in favour of his son. The end would still have been Alexander III, Pobedonostsev, and Katkov.

If the seeds of Alexander's tragedy lay in his personal character and the resulting inability to combine freedom and authority, it is true that unfavourable circumstances made his difficulties almost insuperable. The Tsar was fated to preside over one of the recurring and normally abortive 'liberal' interludes in the history of Russia. After the reign of Nicholas, as after those of Peter I, Paul I, or Stalin, a 'thaw' had become an imperative necessity. The new government must throw off the odium accumulated by the preceding despotism. Yet as soon as Alexander lifted the tight lid of repression, the compressed steam began to escape with powerful effect. Conditions developed enough to frighten even a ruler less naturally insecure than Alexander. Not for nothing did the great Tocqueville observe that the most dangerous moment for a bad government usually comes when it begins to reform itself. By 1862 the dangers of the 'thaw' were clearly apparent to all, and repression, never completely abandoned, again came into its own.

Alexander has been criticized for 'abandoning' his earlier course. Yet what could the Emperor have done? The establishment of a democratic form of freedom was surely out of the question in the conditions of nineteenth-century Russia. Oligarchic rule, as demanded by the disgruntled gentry? Complete freedom for the radical press and its revolutionary supporters? Could the Poles be given their freedom—within the boundaries of 1772 which they claimed? If not, what course was left but repression once Wielopolski's policy had failed? Real freedom in the Russian empire was an impossibility. So, regrettably from Alexander's point of view, was a policy of effective repression—except in Poland and Lithuania after the suppression of the insurrection. Alexander was not by nature a 'stern reactionary' like his father or his son. His hankering after popularity sometimes introduced an element of weakness and hesitation into a repressive system. In any case, the zemstvos and the new courts, supported by the weight of public opinion, made 'black repression' of the type Muraviev and Panin might have favoured a practical impossibility. Finally, except for a time under Shuvalov, the police organization was weak and inefficient. The weapons of the modern totalitarian state were not at the Tsar's disposal. Complete repression was no more practicable than complete freedom. Only a compromise policy was possible.

It is here that the Tsar's course is open to criticism. The compromise to which, under pressure, he consented at the end of his reign might have been greeted with acclamation if it had followed the introduction of the zemstvo and judicial reforms. Instead, frightened by Karakozov's attempt, the Tsar, rather than listen to Valuiev and the Grand-Duke Constantine, handed over power to Shuvalov and Trepov. It was a fateful decision. The wiser course *might*, if adopted, have led

Russia along the road of peaceful constitutional development.

Could Alexander have prevented the Turkish War which finally helped to destroy his system? The conclusion would appear to be that the pressure for warlike action, although powerful, was not irresistible. The Tsar —half-unwillingly—allowed himself to be dragged along the road which might lead to Constantinople. Public opinion did not force him into war; when he made his decision the Pan-Slav agitation had passed its peak. What Alexander hoped for—perhaps understandably—was a military walk-over to bolster up his shaken régime. A century-old ambition of the Russian people might be realized. Osman Pasha's unexpected resistance at Plevna upset the Russian plans. What might have been a brilliant Russian triumph became a disappointing compromise. Circumstances, as well as the flaws in his personal character, were responsible for the failures of Alexander's reign.

And yet even though Alexander cannot be termed a successful ruler, the results of his reign challenge comparison with the more spectacular achievements of Peter the Great and Lenin. The policy of 'modernization' applied to almost every sphere of Russian life made Alexander one of Russia's great 'westernizers'. In his reign, and in no small degree as the result of official policy, the Russian empire passed from the semi-feudal to the early capitalist stage of its development. Far-reaching social changes resulted. In a different sphere, the reforms of Alexander II helped to assure Russia's survival as a major power after her collapse in the Crimean War. Under him, the bounds of the empire were enlarged. Finland and Bulgaria were set on the road to nationhood, the economic and social structure of Poland was transformed. Finally, although Alexander was not himself a distinguished patron of the arts, it was in his reign that Turgeniev, Dostoevsky and Tolstoy, Mussorgsky, Chaikovsky and

Rimsky-Korsakov, wrote and composed their master-pieces. The foundations were being laid for Russia's cultural 'conquests'.

In fact, there was more than a little truth in the remarks made by one French diplomat to another during Alexander's funeral :

"Have a good look at this martyr. He was a great tsar and deserved a kinder fate. . . . His was not a great intellect, but he had a generous soul, very upright and very lofty. He loved his people and his solicitude for the humble and the suffering was unbounded. . . . Remember the reforms he introduced. Peter the Great was the author of none more deeply reaching, and he put into them less of his heart. . . . Think of all the resistance he had to overcome to abolish serfdom and restore the foundation of rural economy. Think that thirty million men owe their affranchisement to him. . . . And his administrative reforms ! He aimed at nothing less than the destruction of the arbitrary bureaucracy and social privilege. In the judicial sphere he established equality before the law, assured the independence of the magistrates, abolished corporal punishment, instituted the jury. And this was done by the immediate successor of the despot Nicholas I ! . . . In foreign politics his work is on the same scale. He followed the line taken by Catherine II on the Black Sea; he wiped out the humiliations of the Treaty of Paris; he brought the eagles of Muscovy to the shores of the Propontis, the very walls of Constantinople; he delivered the Bulgar; he established Russian dominion in the heart of Central Asia. . . . Finally, on the morning of his death, he was working on a reform which would have surpassed all the others, would have launched Russia irrevocably along the track of the modern world: the granting of a parliamentary charter. . . . And the Nihilists have killed him ! . . . But mark the odd coincidence of history, the strange irony of things. Lincoln, the emancipator of the American negroes, was also assassinated. Now, it was the deliverance of the negroes which brought in its train, on the other side of the world, the affranchisement of the *moujiks*. Alexander did not intend that Russia should remain the only serf-holding nation in the Christian world.[1] . . . Oh, a liberator's is a dangerous job!"[2]

[1] de Vogüé is at fault here. Alexander's resolution to free the Russian serfs preceded the abolition of negro slavery in the U.S.A.

[2] M. Paléologue, *The Tragic Romance of Emperor Alexander II* (London, n.d.), pp. 27 ff.

THERE exists no adequate biography of Alexander II in any language. The fullest life is the official biography of S. S. Tatishchev, *Imperator Aleksandr II* (St. Petersburg, 1903, 2 vols.), which, however, suffers from the defects inseparable from the work of a court historian. In English there is a popular biography by S. Graham, *Tsar of Freedom: Life and Reign of Alexander II* (New Haven, 1935). A French diplomat, M. Paléologue, has produced a romanticized account of Alexander's relations with Catherine Dolgoruky (published in English as *The Tragic Romance of the Emperor Alexander II*, London n.d.).

Neither is there an adequate account of Alexander's reforms. G. A. Dzhanshiev's standard work on the subject (*Epokha velikikh Reform*, St. Petersburg, 1907), is little more than a useful quarry. A. A. Golovachev's *Desjatj let reform* (St. Petersburg, 1872), is slight, but interesting as giving the views of a contemporary observer. A. A. Kornilov's *Obshchestvennoe dvizhenie pri Aleksandre II* (Moscow, 1909), contains an analysis of public reaction to the reforms. In English there is a comprehensive study of the liberation of the serfs in G. T. Robinson's *Rural Russia under the Old Regime* (New York and London, 1932). A Leroy-Beaulieu's *Un homme d'état Russe: Nicolas Milutine* (Paris, 1884), remains a useful biography of one of the moving spirits of the reform movement.

Alexander's foreign policy can be studied in several works. Ch. Friese's *Russland und Preussen vom Krimkrieg bis zum Polnischen Aufstand* (Berlin, 1931), is indispensable for the early years of the reign. Relations with France are analysed in F. Charles-Roux's *Alexandre II, Gortchakoff et Napoléon III* (Paris, 1913). Russian policy in the early and middle years of the reign can be studied in W. E. Mosse's *The European Powers and the German Question 1848–1871* (Cambridge, 1958), while the later years are covered in B. H. Sumner's *Russia and the Balkans 1870–1880* (Oxford, 1937).

There are a number of interesting contemporary accounts. The system of Nicholas I is vividly portrayed in *The Memoirs of Alexander Herzen*, translated by J. D. Duff (New Haven, 1923), and in A. de Custine's *La Russie en 1839* (Bruxelles, 1843), edited and translated into English by P. P. Kohler as *Journey for our time: the journals of the Marquis de Custine* (London, 1953). A lively picture of the beginnings of the reign emerges from P. Kropotkin's *Memoirs of a Revolutionist* (London, 1899), and the Prussian diplomat K. v. Schlözer's *Petersburger Briefe* (Stuttgart u. Berlin, 1922). The latter years of the reign are covered by the memoirs of the ultra-conservative Prince V. P. Meshchersky, *Moi Vospominanija* (St. Petersburg, 1898), and the invaluable reminiscences of the German ambassador, General v. Schweinitz, *Denkwürdigkeiten des Botschafters General v. Schweinitz* (Berlin, 1927). Two thoughtful foreign observers produced detailed accounts—D. Mackenzie-Wallace, *Russia* (revised edition, London, 1905), and A. Leroy-Beaulieu, *L'Empire des Tsars et les Russes* (Paris, 1881).

The two leading histories of Russia in a non-Russian language contain admirable surveys of the reign: M. T. Florinsky, *Russia* (New York, 1953, 2 vols.), Vol. II, Chapters XXXIII–XXXVII, and K. Stählin, *Geschichte Russlands* (Königsberg Pr. u. Berlin; completed 1939, 4 vols.), Vol. IV, part 1, Chapters I–IV.

Of works more readily accessible to the British reader, H. Seton-Watson's *The Decline of Imperial Russia* (London, 1952) and Bernard Pares's *A History of Russia* (4th edn., London, 1944) also contain useful accounts of the reign.

# Index